ELEMENTARY KOREAN I

Activity Book

First Edition

Jiyoung Kim, Ph.D.
Indiana University, Bloomington

SAN DIEGO

x

Bassim Hamadeh, CEO and Publisher
Angela Schultz, Senior Field Acquisitions Editor
Alisa Munoz, Project Editor
Alia Bales, Production Editor
Jess Estrella, Senior Graphic Designer
Greg Isales, Licensing Associate
Natalie Piccotti, Director of Marketing
Kassie Graves, Senior Vice President of Editorial
Jamie Giganti, Director of Academic Publishing

3970 Sorrento Valley Blvd., Ste. 500, San Diego, CA 92121

Contents

Introduction. The Korean Alphabet

한글

Objectives

- You will be able to read and write Korean consonants and vowels.
- You will be able to recognize individual Korean consonants and vowels when hearing them.
- You will be able to form a syllable block in Korean.
- You will be able to write your name in Korean.

Korean Vowels 한국어 모음

- 10 vowels: ㅏ, ㅑ, ㅓ, ㅕ, ㅗ, ㅛ, ㅜ, ㅠ, ㅡ, ㅣ
- Compound vowels: ㅐ, ㅒ, ㅔ, ㅖ, ㅘ, ㅝ, ㅚ, ㅙ, ㅞ, ㅟ, ㅢ

Korean Consonants 한국어 자음

- 14 consonants: ㄱ, ㄴ, ㄷ, ㄹ, ㅁ, ㅂ, ㅅ, ㅇ, ㅈ, ㅊ, ㅋ, ㅌ, ㅍ, ㅎ
- Double consonants: ㄲ, ㄸ, ㅃ, ㅆ, ㅉ

Activity 1: Find Vowels of the Words I (Basic Vowels)

Listen to your instructor say the following words, and write the vowels of the words.

a.

ㅋㅐ ㄴ ㄷ

b.

ㅋ ㅍ

c.

ㅊ ㅈ

d.

ㅌ ㄴ ㅅ

e.

ㅇ ㄱ

f.

ㅍ ㅇ ㄴ

Activity 2: Find Vowels of the Words II (Compound Vowels)

Listen to your instructor say the following words, and write the vowels of the words.

a.

ㅇ　ㄷ

b.

ㅇ　ㅇ　ㅍ　ㅇ

c.

ㅋ　ㅇ

d.

ㅇ　ㅇ　ㅌ

e.

ㅇ　플

f.

ㅅ　ㅇ

Activity 3: Write Vowels of the Words I (Basic Vowels)

Listen to your instructor say the following words, and write the vowels of the words.

a.

_____

b.

_____

c.

_____

d.

_____

Activity 4: Write Vowels of the Words II (Compound Vowels)

Listen to your instructor say the following words, and write the vowels of the words.

a.

_____

b.

_____

c.

_____

d.

_____

Activity 5: Find Consonants of the Words I (Basic Consonants)

Listen to your instructor say the following words, and write the consonants of the words.

a.

ㅔ ㅣ ㅡ

b.

ㅣ ㅏ

c.

ㅜ ㅡ

d.

ㅡ ㅏ ㅔ ㅣ

e.

ㅏ ㅣ ㅗ

f.

ㅏ ㅡ ㅡ

Activity 6: Find Consonants of the Words II (Double Consonants)

Listen and write the double consonants in the blank spaces as your instructor says them.

ㄲ, ㄸ, ㅃ, ㅆ, ㅉ

1. 우리 오__ㅏ
2. __ㅏ치__ㅏ치 설날
3. 부부__ㅏ움
4. __ㅏ장면
5. __ㅏ사로운 햇살

Activity 7: Find Consonants of the Words II (Three Series of Stop Consonants)

Listen to your instructor and circle the word you hear.

1. 가지/까지
2. 공/콩
3. 바다/파다
4. 사다/싸다
5. 자다/차다/짜다
6. 파다/따다
7. 모자/포자
8. 줍다/춥다

Activity 8: Play a Card Game of Forming a Syllable Block

Divide into two groups with each group getting one set of consonant cards and vowel cards. Listen and form a syllable by picking a consonant card (or more consonant cards if it includes final consonants) and a vowel card as your instructor says them. The group that forms a syllable and reads it first gets a point.

Activity 9: Write Your Name in Korean

Write your name in Korean on the name card by combining the most appropriate consonant and vowel.

Examples: Emily Jackson: Your name:

에밀리 잭슨

Mark Anderson:

마크 앤더슨

Activity 10: Write Loanwords in Korean

Write the following loanwords in Korean by forming appropriate syllable blocks.

Hamburger	햄버거		
Printer	프린터		
Camera			
Campus			
Building			
Cup			
Lemon			
Computer			
Game			
Boat			
Popcorn			

Cultural Awareness: The Korean Alphabet 한글

한글 is the name of the Korean alphabet, but its original name was not 한글. When King Sejong created the new alphabet in the fifteenth century, he named it 훈민정음, which means "right sounds to educate people." Later, a Korean linguist 주시경 named it 한글 in the early twentieth century and, ever since, the name 한글 has become common. Like English, letters of the 한글 represent individual sounds. 한글 is well known as a very scientific and systematic alphabet, so it has been praised by many linguists and scholars. 한글 is the only alphabet in the world that was created by a single man, and whose inventor and the date of the creation were perfectly documented. Creating a new alphabet alone is an amazing work. No one has ever done such a valuable job before in human history.

Figure 0.1: Statue of King Sejong, the inventor of the Korean alphabet 한글.

Credits

- IMG 0.1a: Source: https://pixabay.com/en/canada-flag-mape-leaf-national-26982/.
- IMG 0.1b: Source: https://pixabay.com/en/coffee-beans-coffee-bean-drink-1117933/.
- IMG 0.1c: Source: https://pixabay.com/en/cheese-cheesy-closeup-close-up-1238395/.
- IMG 0.1d: Source: https://pixabay.com/en/tennis-sports-comic-character-comic-1298769/.
- IMG 0.1e: Source: https://pixabay.com/en/people-woman-yoga-mat-meditation-2557546/.
- IMG 0.1f: Source: https://pixabay.com/images/id-179726/.
- IMG 0.2b: Source: https://pixabay.com/en/wireless-technology-three-dimensional-1967494/.
- IMG 0.2c: Source: https://pixabay.com/en/background-bitter-breakfast-bright-1239438/.
- IMG 0.2d: Source: https://pixabay.com/en/cartoon-character-waiter-idea-2947794/.
- IMG 0.2e: Source: https://pixabay.com/images/id-1262895/.
- IMG 0.2f: Source: https://pixabay.com/images/id-99263/.
- IMG 0.3a: Source: https://pixabay.com/images/id-4775023/.
- IMG 0.3b: Source: https://pixabay.com/images/id-685704/.
- IMG 0.3c: Source: https://pixabay.com/images/id-3231772/.
- IMG 0.3d: Source: https://pixabay.com/images/id-715588/.
- IMG 0.4a: Source: https://pixabay.com/images/id-790220/.
- IMG 0.4b: Source: https://pixabay.com/images/id-642510/.
- IMG 0.4c: Source: https://pixabay.com/images/id-3907119/.
- IMG 0.4d: Copyright © by Noah Sussman (CC BY 2.0) at https://flic.kr/p/4pFrhV
- IMG 0.5a: Source: https://pixabay.com/en/cake-strawberries-2459931/.
- IMG 0.5b: Source: https://pixabay.com/images/id-1081534/.
- IMG 0.5c: Source: https://pixabay.com/images/id-869212/.
- IMG 0.5d: Source: https://pixabay.com/en/pasta-noodles-spagetti-spaghetti-2100171/.
- IMG 0.5e: Source: https://pixabay.com/images/id-4611968/.
- IMG 0.5f: Source: https://pixabay.com/images/id-4898571/
- IMG 0.6: Source: https://pixabay.com/en/tag-label-grey-sale-gift-33551/
- Fig. 0.1: Source: https://pixabay.com/en/king-sejong-the-great-statue-1414289/.

Chapter 1. Introducing Yourself

안녕하세요?

Objectives

- You will be able to greet your classmates and your teacher in Korean.
- You will be able to introduce yourself in Korean to someone you meet for the first time.
- You will be able to ask questions about someone's name, school year, and nationality.
- You will be able to introduce your classmates to the class in Korean.

Key Expressions and Structures

- 안녕하세요?: Hi, Hello, how are you?
- 반갑습니다: Nice to meet you!
- N1 은/는 N2 이에요/예요: N1 is N2.
- N 이/가 뭐예요?: What is N?
- 이름: name, 전공: major, 학년: school year, 공부하다: to study
- 미국 사람: American, 영국 사람: British, 일본 사람: Japanese, 중국 사람: Chinese

Task: Introducing Yourself

Introduce yourself in Korean class on the first day of the semester and get to know each other, including your teacher, by asking about the school year, nationality, and major.

Practice Questions

1. 이름이 뭐예요?
2. 어느 나라 사람이에요?
3. 몇 학년이에요?
4. 전공이 뭐예요?
5. 유진 씨는 한국 사람이에요?

Activity 1: 학기 첫 날 한국어 반 친구에게 인사해 보세요.

Introduce yourself to your classmates on the first day of the semester. Say "hi," your name, and "nice to meet you."

Model Conversation

에밀리:	**안녕하세요?**
	에밀리입니다.
	반갑습니다.
데이빗:	안녕하세요?
	데이빗입니다.
	반갑습니다.
김유진:	안녕하세요?
	김유진입니다.
	반갑습니다.

Your Own Conversation

You:	안녕하세요?
	_____입니다.
	(Your name.)
	반갑습니다.
반 친구 1:	_____
	(Hi.)
	_____입니다.
	반갑습니다.
반 친구 2:	안녕하세요?
	_____입니다.
	_____
	(Nice to meet you.)

Activity 2: 학기 첫 날 선생님께 인사해 보세요.

Introduce yourself to your teacher on the first day of the semester. Say "hello," your name, and "nice to meet you."

Model Conversation

선생님:	안녕하세요?
	한국어 선생님 김지영입니다.
	반갑습니다.
데이빗:	**선생님, 안녕하세요? (With a bow.)**
	데이빗입니다.
	반갑습니다.
김유진:	**선생님, 안녕하세요? (With a bow.)**
	김유진입니다.
	반갑습니다.

Your Own Conversation

선생님:	안녕하세요?
	한국어 선생님 _____입니다.
	(Teacher's name.)
	반갑습니다.
학생 1:	선생님, 안녕하세요? (With a bow.)
	_____입니다.
	반갑습니다.
학생 2:	_____ (With a bow.)
	(Say hi to your teacher!)
	_____입니다.
	_____
	(Nice to meet you.)

Pattern Practice (~은/는)

Talk about the people in the pictures. They are celebrities from several different countries. Tell your partner about ones that you know. Make sure to use the topic particle ~은/는 when talking about them. You may use English words to say their occupation. For example, you can say "베컴은 soccer player 예요" since the word for soccer player is new to a beginner.

CELEBRITIES:

1.

테일러 스위프트**는**
가수(singer)**예요**.

미국 사람**이에요**.

2.

김연아**는**

_____

_____

_____

3.

_____

_____

_____

_____

4.

_____

_____

_____

_____

5.

_____

_____

_____

_____

6.

_____

_____

_____

_____

Activity 3: 한국어 수업 첫 날 반 친구의 학년, 국적, 전공에 대해 물어 보세요.

Ask your classmates their school year, nationality, and major on the first day of Korean class.

Model Conversation

리에: 안녕하세요? 저는 리에 장이에요.

유진: 안녕하세요? 저는 김유진예요.

리에 & 유진: 반갑습니다.

리에: 유진 씨는 **어느 나라**[1] **사람**이에요?

유진: 저는 한국 사람이에요.

리에: 아, 그래요? 저는 중국 사람이에요.

유진: 리에 씨는 **몇**[2] **학년**이에요?

리에: 저는 1 학년이에요.

유진: 아, 그래요? 저도 1 학년이에요.

리에: 유진 씨는 **전공 (major)**이 뭐예요?

유진: 저는 한국어 공부해요.

리에: 아, 그래요? 저는 생물학 (biology) 공부해요.

---

[1] 어느 나라: which country
[2] 몇: what, which, how many/much

Your Own Conversation

A: _____   _____

          (Hi.)   (Your name.)

B: _____   _____

          (Hi.)   (Your name.)

A & B   _____

          (Nice to meet you.)

A: _____ 씨는 **어느 나라 사람이에요?**

B: _____

A: 아, 그래요? 저도/는 _____이에요/예요.

B: _____ 씨는 **몇 학년이에요?**

A: _____

B: 아, 그래요? 저는/도 _____이에요/예요.

A: _____ 씨는 **전공이 뭐예요?**

B: 저는 _____ 공부해요.

A: 아, 그래요? 저는 _____ 공부해요.

Activity 4: 한국어 반 친구를 소개해 보세요.

Interview three classmates about their name, school year, nationality, and major. Introduce them to the class. Take notes of your interview in the table below.

Interview Questions

1. 이름이 뭐예요?

2. 몇 학년이에요?

3. 어느 나라 사람이에요?

4. 전공이 뭐예요?

Model Report

이름	학년	국적 (nationality)	전공
친구 1. 김유진	1 학년	한국	한국어
친구 2. 에밀리 잭슨	1 학년	미국	국제학[3]
친구 3. 리에 장	3 학년	중국	생물학

유진 씨는 인디애나 대학교 1 학년이에요. 한국 사람이에요.

전공은 한국어예요. 에밀리 씨도 인디애나 대학교 1 학년이에요. 미국 사람이에요.

국제학을 공부해요. 리에 씨는 인디애나 대학교 3 학년이에요. 중국 사람이에요.

생물학을 공부해요.

---

[3] 국제학: international studies

Your Report

이름	학년	국적 (nationality)	전공
친구 1.			
친구 2.			
친구 3.			

_____

_____

_____

_____

_____

_____

Cultural Awareness: Taking a Bow When Greeting 인사하기

Greeting is very important in Korean culture. You'll be considered well-educated just by greeting people appropriately in Korea. Another important thing about greeting is taking a bow. Most of the time, greeting in Korean culture involves a bow.

Normally, when you bow to teachers or elders, lower your waist and shoulders by 30 degrees.

In a very casual meeting with your acquaintances, colleagues, and not-so-close friends, just nod your head. Sometimes, if you don't want to talk or you don't have anything to talk about, then just nod.

In a formal setting, when you say thank you in front of a group of people, decline by 45 degrees.

Try to get used to bowing, at least to your Korean teacher!

Figure 1.1: Taking a bow when greeting in Korea.

Credits

Chapter 2. Talking about Your Belongings

노트북 있으세요?

Objectives

- You will be able to say what kinds of items you have, such as a laptop, a cellphone, a bag, a dictionary, an umbrella, or a watch.
- You will be able to ask a question to find out what kind of items your classmates possess.
- You will be able to write a paragraph about your classmates' belongings.

Key Expressions and Structures

- N 이/가 있어요?/있으세요?: Do you have N?
- ~(으)세요: Honorific ending
- N 이/가 있어요/없어요: I (don't) have/possess an N.
- 노트북: laptop, 시계: watch, 가방: bag, 모자: cap, 사전: dictionary, 헤드폰: headphones, 아이 패드: iPad, 텀블러: tumbler

Task: Talking about Items That You Have

Say the items you have, and find out what kind of items your classmates possess.

Practice Questions

1. OO 씨는 노트북이 **있어요**?
2. 아이 패드도 **있어요**?
3. 선생님은 아이폰이 **있으세요**?
4. 맥북도 **있으세요**?

Pattern Practice 1(~이/가 있어요?)

Pair up with another classmate, and tell each other which items belong to whom in the picture below. Write the person's name in the blank. For example, you first say "에밀리 씨는 가방이 있어요," then your partner finds the item in the picture and writes the name in the blank. (Go to Appendix A. One person gets Picture 1 on page 123 and the other Picture 2 on page 125.)

Pattern Practice 2(~이/가 있으세요?)

Ask your teacher and find out what kind of items they have in the picture below. Make sure to use the honorific ending ~이/가 있으세요? when asking your teacher. For example, you can ask "선생님, 아이폰이 있으세요?" and mark the items your teacher has.

_____ _____ _____ _____ _____ _____

_____ _____ _____ _____ _____ _____

Activity 1: 어떤 소지품을 가지고 있는지 친구에게 물어 보세요.

Pair up with a classmate, and ask your partner if they possess items like the latest iPhone, iPad, laptop, or K-pop CD, for example.

Model Conversation 1

김유진:	에밀리 씨, 맥북[4] 있으세요?
에밀리:	네, 있어요.
김유진:	아이 패드도 있으세요?
에밀리:	아니요, 아이 패드는 없어요.

Model Conversation 2

에밀리:	유진 씨, 빅뱅[5] CD 있으세요?
김유진:	아니요, 없어요.
에밀리:	그럼, BTS[6] CD 는 있으세요?
김유진:	네, BTS CD 는 있어요.

Your Own Conversation

A: _____ 씨, _____ 있어요?

(Ask if they have an item.)

B: 네/아니요, _____.

A: _____도/은/는 있어요?

(Ask if they have another item.)

B: 네, _____도/은/는 있어요. /아니요, _____도/은/는 없어요.

    (Yes, I have.)   (No, I don't have.)

---

[4] 맥북: MacBook
[5] 빅뱅 is a famous K-pop group.
[6] BTS is a famous K-pop group.

Activity 2: 한국어 반 친구들이 어떤 물건을 가지고 있어요?

Interview three classmates about their belongings. You can choose any items you'd like to ask about. Take notes of your interview in the table below. Report what kind of items they have and who has something unique.

	e.g. 에밀리	친구 1.	친구 2.	친구 3.
Item 1.	맥북 에어			
Item 2.	아이 패드 (X)			
Item 3.	아이폰 11			
Item 4.				
Item 5.				

Model Report

에밀리 씨는 맥북 에어가 있어요. 아이폰 11 도 있어요. 그런데 아이 패드는 없어요.

유진 씨는 BTS CD 가 있어요. Exo CD 도 있어요. 그런데 빅뱅 CD 는 없어요.

마크 씨는 한국어 책이 있어요. 영어 책도 있어요. 그런데 중국어 책은 없어요.

Your Report

_____

_____

_____

_____

Cultural Awareness: Using the Honorific 존댓말

Using the honorific is closely related to Korean culture, showing respect and politeness toward others, especially the elders. When using the honorific, you should consider many things, such as one's age, social status, and closeness and intimacy with you. People might feel insulted when you don't properly use the honorific in Korea. Your Korean will be recognized as being at a superior level when you feel comfortable using the honorific.

Figure 2.1. Respect.

Credits

Chapter 3. Describing How You Feel about Your Classes

한국어 수업이 어때요?

Objectives

- You will be able to ask and answer questions about a course you take this semester: how you like the class, who the professor is, how you like them, and what your classmates are like.
- You will be able to write a paragraph about a course you take.
- You will be able to describe how you feel about your school, the place you live in, and your roommates.

Key Expressions and Structures

- N 이/가 어때요?: How is N? (How do you feel about N?)
- V ~어/아요: Polite ending
- N 은/는 누구세요?/누구예요?: Who is N?
- 한국어 반: Korean class, 반 친구들: classmates, 생물학: biology, 기숙사: dorm, 룸메이트: roommate, 방: room, 어렵다: difficult, 깨끗하다: clean, 친절하다: kind

Task: Describing How You Feel about Classes You Take This Semester

Describe how you feel about the classes you take and your professors, and ask questions to find out how your classmates feel about them.

Practice Questions

1. OO 대학교가 **어때요?** 캠퍼스가 커요?
2. 한국어 수업이 **어때요?** 선생님은 **누구세요?** 반 친구들은 **어때요?**
3. 기숙사가 **어때요?** 방이 넓어요?
4. 룸메이트가 **어때요?** 친절해요?

Pattern Practice 1. (~이/가 어때요?)

Look at the pictures below and ask your partner what they think. Make sure to use polite style ~ 어/아요 when answering.

1.

   A: 교실이 어때요?

   B: 사람들이 아주 많아요.

2.

   _____

   _____

3.

   _____

   _____

4.

   _____

   _____

5.

   _____

   _____

6.

   _____

   _____

Pattern Practice 2. (~이/가 어때요?)

How do you like your school, your dorm, the school cafeteria, and your roommates? Ask your partner the following questions and make a dialogue about each topic.

Model Dialogue

A: 인디애나 대학교가 어때요?

B: 아주 좋아요.

A: 캠퍼스가 커요?

B: 네, 아주 커요. 캠퍼스가 정말 예뻐요.[7]

Your Dialogues

_____

_____

_____

_____

_____

_____

---

[7] 예뻐요: pretty

Activity 1: 한국어 수업에 대해서 말해 보세요.

How do you like your Korean class? Pair up with another classmate, and ask each other questions about Korean class. Describe how you like the class, who the professor is, how you like them, what your classmates are like, and where the classroom is.

Model Conversation

제임스:	**한국어 수업이 어때요?**
에밀리:	아주 재미있어요.
제임스:	**선생님은 누구세요?**
에밀리:	김지영 선생님이세요. 아주 좋으세요.
제임스:	**한국어 반 친구들은 어때요?**
에밀리:	반 친구들도 아주 좋아요. 같이 매일 한국어를 공부해요.
제임스:	한국어 수업 교실은 어디 있어요?
에밀리:	SGIS 빌딩 1 층에 있어요.

Your Own Conversation

A: 한국어 수업이 _____?

(Ask how your partner feels about Korean class.)

B: _____. 그리고/그런데 _____.

A: 선생님은 _____?

(Ask who the professor is.)

B: _____ 선생님이세요. _____.

(Say how you feel about them.)

A: 한국어 반 학생들은 _____?

(Ask how your partner feels about the classmates.)

B: _____. 그리고/그런데 _____.

A: 교실은 어디 있어요?

B: _____.

Activity 2: 이번 학기에 듣고 있는 수업에 대해서 말해 보세요.

How do you like classes you are taking this semester? Choose one class (other than Korean class) that you are taking this semester and talk about it. Describe how you like the class, who the professor is, how you like them, what your classmates are like, and where the classroom is.

Model Conversation

에밀리:	데이빗 씨, 오늘 수업 있으세요?
데이빗:	네, 생물학 수업이 있어요.
에밀리:	**생물학 수업이 어때요?**
데이빗:	아주 재미있어요. 그런데 어려워요.[8] 그래서 매일 공부해요.
에밀리:	**선생님은 누구세요?**
데이빗:	마크 앤더슨 선생님이세요. 아주 친절하세요.[9]
에밀리:	**생물학 반 친구들은 어때요?**
데이빗:	아주 좋아요. 저는 유진 씨하고 친해요.[10]
에밀리:	아, 그래요? 교실은 어디 있어요?
데이빗:	사이언스 (science) 빌딩 3 층에 있어요.

Your Own Conversation

A: _____ 씨, 오늘 수업 있으세요?

B: 네, _____ 수업이 있어요.

(A course you are taking.)

A: _____ 어때요?

(Ask how your partner feels about the class.)

B: _____. 그리고/그런데 _____.

---

[8] 어렵다: to be difficult, hard
[9] 친절하다: to be kind, friendly
[10] 친하다: to be close (to someone)

A: 선생님은 _____?

                  (Ask who the professor of the class is.)

B: _____ 선생님이세요. _____.

                                                      (How you feel about the professor.)

A: _____ 반 친구들은 어때요?

B: _____.

A: 교실은 어디 있어요?

B: _____.

Activity 3: 이번 학기에 듣고 있는 수업에 대해서 써 보세요.

Write about the class you talked about for Activity 2 above. Include how you like the class, who the professor is, how you like the professor, how your classmates are, and where the classroom is.

Model Report

이번 학기[11] 저는 생물학을 공부해요. 아주 재미있어요. 그런데 조금 어려워요. 그래서 매일 생물학을 공부해요. 선생님은 마크 앤더슨 선생님이세요. 아주 친절하세요. 생물학 반에 학생들이 많아요. 저는 데이빗 씨하고 아주 친해요. 같이 도서관에서 공부해요. 교실은 사이언스 빌딩 3 층에 있어요.

Your Report

_____

_____

_____

_____

_____

---

[11] 이번 학기: this semester

Cultural Awareness: The Education System in Korea 한국의 교육

The school system in Korea is divided into 초등학교 (elementary school), 중학교 (middle school), 고등학교 (high school), and 대학교 (university). Students spend six years at 초등학교, three years at 중학교, another three years at 고등학교, and four years at 대학교. Unlike schools in the United States, the academic year of Korean schools begins in March and ends in February. Thus, it is divided into four terms: the spring semester (March to June), the summer vacation (July to August), the fall semester (September to December), and the winter vacation (January to February).

A unique feature of education in Korea is that private educational institutes called 학원 play an important part in it. Most students, including college students, go to more than one 학원 after school. The types of 학원 are diverse, ranging from math to English, music, sports, and arts. It can be said that students work double shifts, so they have a tight schedule every day from 7:00 a.m. until late at night. It is interesting that there are few public school buses in Korea, but you will see a lot of 학원 buses running everywhere in Korea. You can find 학원, like the one shown in the picture below, on almost every block in any town in Korea.

Figure 3.1: 학원 in Korea.

Credits

- IMG 3.1a: Source: https://pixabay.com/images/id-105709/.
- IMG 3.1b: Copyright © by AntMan3001 (CC BY-SA 2.0) at https://flic.kr/p/25aoyFQ.
- IMG 3.1c: Copyright © by William F. Yurasko (CC BY 2.0) at https://flic.kr/p/8V7Jio.
- IMG 3.1d: Copyright © by missbossy (CC BY 2.0) at https://flic.kr/p/5a1VDN.
- IMG 3.1e: Source: https://pixabay.com/images/id-3068617/.
- IMG 3.1f: Source: https://pixabay.com/images/id-2610863/.
- Fig. 3.1: Copyright © by Steve Slep () at https://www.flickr.com/photos/steveslep/2172976741/.

Chapter 4. Identifying the Location of Place

기숙사가 어디에 있어요?

Objectives

- You will be able to identify the location of an entity and specify further with a position noun indicating front and back, upper and lower, inside and outside, and next to.
- You will be able to ask a question about the location of facilities that you are looking for, such as a dormitory, cafeteria, laundry room, gym, and computer lab.
- You will be able to describe your room and where the objects are placed in the room.

Key Expressions and Structures

- N 이/가 어디에 있어요?: Where is N?
- [Place]에 뭐가 있어요?: What is there in the place?
- N 이/가 [Place]에 있어요: N is in the place.
- N1 이/가 N2 옆/앞/뒤/위/밑에 있어요: N1 is next to/in front of/in the back of/on top of/below N2.

Task: Identifying the Location of School Facilities

You will go to the dormitory that you will move into as a freshman and ask your roommate what kind of facilities there are in the dormitory and the location of them.

Practice Questions

1. 기숙사가 **어디 있어요**?
2. 캠퍼스에 서점이 **어디에 있어요**?
3. 한국어 교실이 **어디에 있어요**?
4. 방 안에 **뭐가 있어요**?

Pattern Practice 1. (~에 있어요.)

Ask your partner about the location of the major cities of the United Staes in the box below. Make sure to use the pattern ~에 있어요.

엘에이, 시카고, 뉴욕, 샌프란시스코, 시애틀, 휴스턴, 라스 베가스, 아틀랜타, 보스턴, 마이애미, 인디애나폴리스, 호놀룰루, 달라스

Model Pattern

A: 엘에이는 **어디에 있어요?**

B: 캘리포니아에 **있어요.**

_____

_____

Pattern Practice 2. (~에 있어요.)

Ask your partner about the location of the universities in the box below. Make sure to use the pattern ~에 있어요.

하버드 대학교, 스탠포드 대학교, 서울 대학교, 옥스포드 대학교, 콜롬비아 대학교, 에모리 대학교, 퍼듀 대학교, 조지타운 대학교

Model Pattern

A: 인디애나 대학교는 **어디에 있어요?**

B: 블루밍턴에 **있어요.**

_____

_____

Pattern Practice 3. (위/옆/앞/뒤에 있어요)

Below is a seating chart of a Korean class. Ask each other where the classmates are seated. Make sure to practice the position nouns 위/옆/앞/뒤.

Model Pattern

A: 에밀리 씨는 **어디에 있어요?**

B: 마크 씨 **옆에 있어요.**

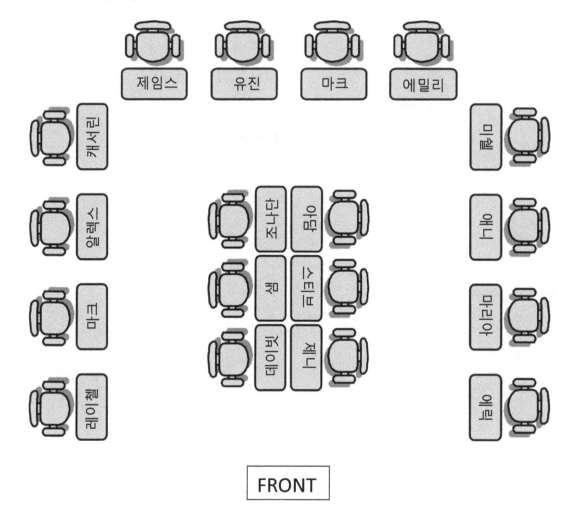

Figure 4.1: Seating chart of a Korean class.

Activity 1: 캠퍼스에 어떤 시설들이 있는지 첫 날 룸메이트에게 물어 보세요.

You are a freshman and just moved into the school dormitory. You meet your roommate and ask them what kind of places and facilities are there on campus, such as the dormitory, library, cafeteria, and bookstore, and where they are located. Suppose that your roommate is a sophomore and familiar with campus.

Model Conversation

김유진:	안녕하세요? 저는 김유진이에요.
룸메이트:	네, 유진 씨? 저는 에밀리예요. 반갑습니다.
김유진:	네, 반갑습니다.
	캠퍼스에 서점이 **어디에 있어요?**
룸메이트:	학생회관 1 층**에 있어요.**
김유진:	캠퍼스에 우체국도 있어요?
룸메이트:	아니요. 우체국은 없어요.

Your Own Conversation

A: _____ 씨, 안녕하세요? _____

룸메이트: 네, 안녕하세요. _____ 반갑습니다.

A: 네, 반갑습니다.

        캠퍼스에 _____이/가 어디 있어요?

        (A place/facility on campus.)

룸메이트: _____.

A: 캠퍼스에 _____도 있어요?

        (Ask if there is another place or facility on campus, too.)

룸메이트: 네/아니요. _____.

Activity 2: 여러분 방 안 책상 위에 있는 물건과 그 위치를 말해 보세요.

Bring a picture of your room, or you may draw your room on a notepad. Describe your room, including where the objects are placed in the room.

Figure 4.2: Objects on the desk.

Model Report

방 안에 책상이 있어요. 책상 위에 컴퓨터하고 책이 있어요. 책은 컴퓨터 옆에 있어요. 컴퓨터 옆에 화분[12]도 있어요. 키보드가 컴퓨터 앞에 있어요. 키보드 앞에는 핸드폰하고 마우스가 있어요. 키보드 옆에는 공책[13]이 있어요. 공책 옆에는 볼펜이 있어요.

Your Report

_____

_____

_____

_____

_____

---

[12] 화분: flower pot
[13] 공책: notepad

Activity 3: 친구에게 방 안 물건의 위치를 말해 주고 그림을 그려 보게 하세요.

Describe your room to your partner looking at the picture that you brought (for Activity 2) and have them draw your room as you described it.

Cultural Awareness: The Boarding House 하숙집

College students in Korea live in various types of housing, such as an apartment, school dormitory, boarding house, or with parents or relatives. The reason why there are more different types of housing for college students in Korea is that the school dormitories are too small to accommodate them. Things are getting better now compared to the past, yet still only a small number of students are lucky enough to live on campus. As a consequence, it is a big deal for a student to find a place to live. You can see a lot of students looking for a place by the time the school semester starts, as seen in the picture below.

The most popular type of housing in the past was a boarding house "하숙집," where meals and other services (cleaning, landry, etc.) are included, depending on its owner. Usually the owner of the boarding house lives together with the students and provides the services; naturally, students develop a very good relationship with the owner even after graduating from the college and leaving the boarding house. Also, the students living in the same boarding house have close friendships and sometimes get together as couples.

Nowadays, the number of boarding houses in Korea has decreased as more apartments have been built since the 1980s. Recently, however, a Korean drama titled *응답하라 1994*, a story of college students in the same boarding house, has been such a big hit that the number of students looking for boarding houses has been temporarily on the rise.

Figure 4.3: Students looking at classified ads for 하숙집.

Credits

- Fig. 4.1: Source: https://pixabay.com/images/id-36512/.
- Fig. 4.2: Source: https://pixabay.com/en/workplace-imac-desktop-creative-3236523/.
- Fig. 4.3: Source: http://www.newsway.kr/view.php?tp=1&ud=2015010915424025507.
- IMG 4.1: Source: https://pixabay.com/en/buy-me-a-coffee-pencil-composition-3067238/.

Chapter 5. Talking about Your Daily Activities

오늘 뭐 해요?

Objectives

- You will be able to ask and answer a question to find out what a person is doing now.
- You will be able to report basic activities you usually do on weekends, such as meeting friends, drinking coffee, or going to see a movie.
- You will be able to say and write about your daily routines, such as eating breakfast/lunch/dinner, taking a class, and studying at a library.

Key Expressions and Structures

- N 은/는 지금 뭐 해요?: What is N doing now?
- ~을/를: Object marker, ~에서: (Dynamic) location marker
- 주말에 뭐 하세요?: What do you do on weekends?
- 오늘: today, 오전: morning, 오후: afternoon, 저녁: evening
- 수업을 듣다: to take a class, 아침/점심/저녁을 먹다: to eat breakfast/lunch/dinner, 친구를 만나다: to meet a friend, 숙제를 하다: to do homework, 영화/텔레비전을 보다: to see/watch a movie/TV, 커피를 마시다: to drink coffee

Task: Talking about Your Daily Routines and Weekend Activities

Ask your friends what they usually do on school days and weekends.

Practice Questions

1. 주말에 보통 **뭐 하세요?**
2. 오늘 오후에 **뭐 하세요?**
3. **어디에서** 한국어 수업**을 들어요?**
4. 보통 **어디에서** 점심**을 먹어요?**
5. 보통 **어디에서 공부해요?**

Pattern Practice: 그림에 있는 사람들이 뭐 하고 있는지 말해 보세요.

Pair up with another classmate, and tell each other what the person in the picture is doing. Write the person's name in the blank. For example, you first say "에밀리 씨는 책을 읽어요," then your partner finds who Emily is and writes the name in the picture. (Go to Appendix B. One person gets Picture 1 on page 127 and the other Picture 2 on page 129.)

_____ _____ _____ _____ _____

_____ _____ _____ _____ _____

_____ _____ _____ _____ _____

Activity 1: 주말에 보통 뭐 하는지 반 친구들에게 물어 보세요.

Talk about what you usually do on weekends.

Model Conversation

김유진: 에밀리 씨, **주말에 보통 뭐 하세요?**

에밀리: 보통 주말 아침에 운동을 해요. 그리고 친구를 만나요.

김유진: 친구하고 **보통 뭐 해요?**

에밀리: 영화를 자주 봐요. 유진 씨는 **주말에 보통 뭐 하세요?**

김유진: 저는 보통 주말에 룸메이트하고 같이 음식을 만들어요.

에밀리: 아, 그래요?

김유진: 그리고 같이 방을 청소해요.

Your Own Conversation

A: _____ 씨, 주말에 보통 뭐 하세요?

B: _____. 그리고 _____.

A: 아, 그래요?

B: _____ 씨는 주말에 보통 뭐 하세요?

A: _____. 그리고 _____.

B: 아, 그래요?

A: 그리고 _____.

    (One more activity you usually do on weekends.)

Activity 2: 보통 학교에서의 하루 일과에 대해서 친구하고 이야기 해 보세요.

Interview your partner about their daily routine on school days, and report it to the class. Take notes of their activities in the table below.

Interview Questions

1. 오전에 뭐 하세요? 수업 있어요?
2. 어디에서 점심 먹어요?
3. 오후에 뭐 하세요?
4. 저녁에 기숙사에서 뭐해요?

Model Report: <u>Emily's</u> Daily Routines

오전	1. 학교에 가요
	2. SGIS 빌딩에서 한국어 수업을 들어요.
	3. 도서관에서 친구를 만나요.
오후	1. 학교 식당에서 친구하고 점심을 먹어요.
	2. 사이언스 빌딩에서 생물학 수업을 들어요.
	3. 도서관에서 공부 해요.
	4. 피아노 수업 들으러 가요.
저녁	1. 기숙사에 가요.
	2. 기숙사 식당에서 저녁을 먹어요.
	3. 한국어 숙제해요.
	4. 룸메이트하고 한국 드라마를 봐요.

에밀리 씨는 오전에 SGIS 빌딩에서 한국어 수업을 들어요. 그리고 도서관에서 친구를 만나요. 학교 식당에서 친구하고 점심을 먹어요. 오후에는 사이언스 빌딩에서 생물학 수업을 들어요. 그리고 도서관에서 공부해요. 그리고 피아노 수업 들으러 가요. 저녁에 기숙사에 가요. 기숙사 식당에서 저녁을 먹어요. 그리고 한국어 숙제해요. 그리고 룸메이트하고 한국 드라마를 봐요.

Your Report: _____'s Daily Routines

오전	1.
	2.
	3.
	4.
오후	1.
	2.
	3.
	4.
저녁	1.
	2.
	3.
	4.

Your Report

_____

_____

_____

_____

_____

_____

Cultural Awareness: College Life in Korea 한국의 대학 생활

It is well known that entering top universities in Korea is very competitive. So, students have to work really hard during their high school years to pass the college entrance exam in Korea. Once they enter a university, everyone strives to fully enjoy their college life as if to make up for the time they were unable to enjoy in high school. Social interactions at social circles/clubs 동아리 활동 and going out on a blind date 소개팅 are the activities that the majority of students especially enjoy during their college years. In Korea, it is very common that your friends introduce you to their friend/acquaintance for the purpose of maybe making it a date.

Figure 5.1: Blind date 소개팅.

Credits

Chapter 6. Asking about the Price of Items

한국어 교과서가 얼마예요?

Objectives

- You will be able to count in Sino-Korean numbers.
- You will be able to use appropriate noun counters for Sino-Korean numbers.
- You will be able to ask and answer the price of books you'd like to buy at a bookstore.
- You will be able to talk about where you live and the rent for the place.
- You will be able to ask and answer when someone's birthday is.

Key Expressions and Structures

- 1–10 (Sino-Korean numbers): 일, 이, 삼, 사, 오, 육, 칠, 팔, 구, 십
- N 이/가 얼마예요?: How much is N?
- N 이/가 몇 층에 있어요?: What floor is N on?
- 생일이 언제예요?: When is your birthday?
- 오늘이 며칠이에요?: What is the date today?
- 생일: birthday, 년: year, 월: month, 일: day, 원: Korean currency, 달러/불: dollar

Task: Buying a Book at a Bookstore

Go to a bookstore and ask about the price of a book you want to purchase.

Practice Questions

1. 한국어 교과서**가 얼마예요**?
2. **몇 학년**이에요?
3. 생일이 **언제예요**?
4. 방이 **몇 층에 있어요**?
5. 오늘이 **며칠이에요**?

Pattern Practice 1. (~이/가 얼마예요?)

Practice how to say the price of the items. Ask your partner about the price of the items on the market flyer, below. Make sure to use the Sino-Korean number when saying the price.

Model pattern

A: 토마토가 **얼마예요?**

B: 사불 구십구**센트**예요.

Pattern Practice 2. (~이/가 언제예요/며칠이에요?)

Ask your partner when the special days are in the box and write its corresponding month in the picture. Be sure to use the appropriate counters for month and day.

> Christmas Day, New Year's Day, Independence Day, Valentine's Day, Mother's Day, Labor Day, Easter Day, Holloween Day, Thanksgiving Day, and Birthday

Model Pattern

A: 크리스마스가 언제예요?/며칠이에요?

B: 십이월 이십오일이에요.

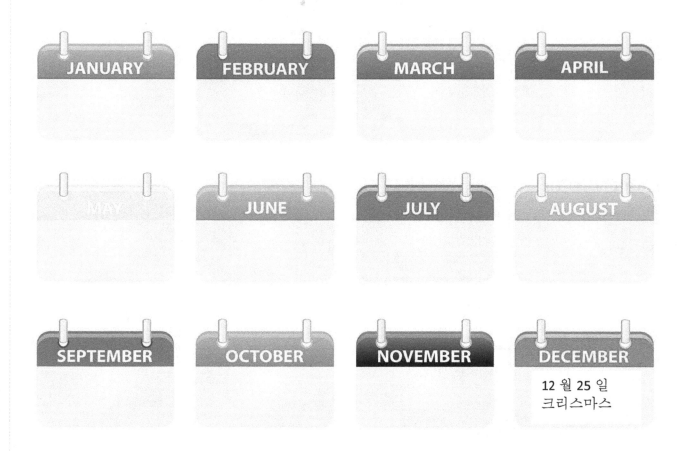

12 월 25 일
크리스마스

Activity 1: 서점에 가서 이번 학기에 듣는 과목 교과서와 워크북, 부교재 등을 사 보세요.

Go to a bookstore to buy a textbook and a supplement. Ask about their prices.

Model Conversation

직 원[14]:	어서 오세요. 뭐 찾으세요?
데이빗:	한국어 1 학년 교과서 있어요?
직 원:	네, 있어요.
데이빗:	**한국어 교과서가 얼마예요?**
직 원:	35 불이에요.
데이빗:	워크북(workbook)도 있어요?
직 원:	네, 워크북은 30 불이에요.
데이빗:	그럼, 교과서하고 워크북 주세요.
직 원:	네, 알겠습니다. 모두[15] 65 불이에요.

Your Own Conversation

직 원:	어서 오세요. 뭐 찾으세요?
학 생:	_____ 있어요?
	(A textbook you are going to buy.)
직 원:	네, 있어요.
학 생:	_____?
	(How much is it?)
직 원:	_____이에요.
	(Say the price.)

---

[14] 직 원: sales clerk
[15] 모두: total

학 생:	워크북/부교재[16]도 있어요?
직 원:	네, 있어요. _____이에요.

(Say the price.)

학 생:	그럼, 교과서하고 워크북/부교재 주세요.
직 원:	네, 알겠습니다. 모두 _____이에요.

(Total price.)

Activity 2: 어디에 사는지 물어보고 렌트가 얼마인지 물어 보세요.

Ask your classmate where they live and how much the rent is.

Model Conversation

김유진:	데이빗 씨, 아파트에 살아요, 기숙사에 살아요?
데이빗:	저는 기숙사에 살아요.
김유진:	기숙사 방이 **몇 층에 있어요?**
데이빗:	3 층에 있어요.
김유진:	방이 좋아요?
데이빗:	네, 아주 좋아요. 그리고 렌트도 아주 싸요.
김유진:	**렌트가 얼마예요?**
데이빗:	550 불이에요.

Your Own Conversation

A:	_____ 씨, 아파트에 살아요, 기숙사에 살아요?
B:	저는 _____에 살아요.
A:	_____?
	(Ask what floor their room is on.)
B:	_____에 있어요.
A:	방이 좋아요?

---

[16] 부교재: auxiliary textbook, supplement

B: 네/아니요, _____. 그리고 렌트가/도 _____.

(Say if the rent is cheap or expensive.)

A: 렌트가 _____?

(How much is the rent?)

B: _____이에요.

Activity 3: 친구의 학년, 생일, 전화 번호, 방 층, 렌트비에 대해서 인터뷰해 보세요.

Interview three classmates about their school year, birthday, phone number, the floor of the place they live in, and the rent, and then report it to the class. Take notes of your interview in the table below. Be sure to use the appropriate counters for Sino-Korean numbers.

Interview Questions

1. _____ 씨, 몇 **학년**이에요?

2. 생일이 **언제예요**?

3. 전화 번호가 뭐예요?

4. 어디에 살아요? 기숙사/아파트 방이 몇 **층**에 있어요?

5. 기숙사/아파트 렌트가 **얼마예요**?

	e.g. 에밀리	친구 1:	친구 2:	친구 3:
1. 학년	1 학년			
2. 생일	4 월 7 일			
3. 전화번호	812-123-4567			
4. 방 층	2 층			
5. 렌트	550 달러			

Model Report

에밀리 씨는 일학년이에요. 생일이 사월 칠일이에요. 전화번호가 팔일이-일이삼-사오육칠이에요. 기숙사에 살아요. 방이 이층에 있어요. 렌트가 싸요. 오백오십 달러예요.

Your Report

_____

_____

_____

_____

Cultural Awareness: Korean Group Game 삼육구 (3.6.9)

Koreans like to play a game when they have a gathering. Among many games, 삼육구 게임 is the most popular group game in Korea. 삼육구 are the Sino-Korean numbers 3, 6, and 9. Most Koreans know how to play the game because its rules are simple as well as fun.

Let's play the 삼육구 game! Form a group of four or more people and play the game. You need to count the Sino-Korean numbers in order to play this game.

Game Rules

1. Each person calls out the Sino-Korean numbers in order 일(1), 이(2), 삼(3), 사(4), 오(5), and so on.
2. Whenever your number is a number including 삼(3), 육(6), or 구(9), you have to clap instead of saying the number.
3. If there are two digits and both include the number 삼(3), 육(6), or 구(9), then you have to clap twice. (e.g., 36: clap twice)

Figure 6.1: Playing 삼육구 Game.

Credits

- IMG 6.1a: Source: https://pixabay.com/images/id-2449019/.
- IMG 6.1b: Source: https://pixabay.com/images/id-2918620/.
- IMG 6.1c: Copyright © by RyanHung (CC BY-SA 2.0) at https://flic.kr/p/dJeiof.
- IMG 6.1d: Source: https://pixabay.com/images/id-1287100/.
- IMG 6.1e: Source: https://pixabay.com/images/id-490474/.
- IMG 6.1f: Source: https://pixabay.com/images/id-1280859/.
- IMG 6.1g: Source: https://pixabay.com/images/id-4126919/.
- IMG 6.1h: Source: https://pixabay.com/images/id-1721633/.
- IMG 6.1i: Source: https://pixabay.com/images/id-4059957/.
- IMG 6.1j: Source: https://pixabay.com/images/id-499068/.
- IMG 6.1k: Source: https://pixabay.com/photos/supermarket-malaysia-834201/.
- IMG 6.1l: Source: https://flic.kr/p/6sADsY.
- IMG 6.1m: Copyright © by Chris Gladis (CC BY-ND 2.0) at https://flic.kr/p/3JYWcm.
- IMG 6.1n: Source: https://flic.kr/p/6sADnU.
- IMG 6.1o: Source: https://flic.kr/p/6swuK4.
- IMG 6.2: Source: https://pixabay.com/images/id-925109/.
- Fig. 6.1: Source: https://pixabay.com/en/meeting-conference-people-table-152506/

Chapter 7. Talking about the Number of Your Belongings

한국어 책이 몇 권 있어요?

Objectives

- You will be able to count native Korean numbers.
- You will be able to use the appropriate noun counter for the native Korean numbers.
- You will be able to say the number of your belongings with an appropriate noun counter.
- You will be able to ask a question to find out how many items/pets/roommates/brothers and sisters/books someone has.

Key Expressions and Structures

- 1–10 (Native Korean number)
  : 하나(1), 둘(2), 셋(3), 넷(4), 다섯(5), 여섯(6), 일곱(7), 여덟(8), 아홉(9), 열(10)
- N 이/가 몇 개 있어요?: How many items do you have?
- N 이/가 몇 마리 있어요?: How many pets (dogs, cats, etc.) do you have?
- N 이/가 몇 명 있어요?: How many people (siblings, roommates, etc.) do you have?
- N 이/가 몇 권 있어요?: How many books do you have?

Task: Talking about the Number of Your Belongings

Ask each other about the number of pets, siblings, books, roommates, and so forth you have.

Practice Questions

1. 한국어 책이 **몇 권 있어요?**
2. 한국어 반에 학생이 **몇 명 있어요?**
3. 캠퍼스에 도서관이 **몇 개 있어요?**
4. 룸메이트 있어요? **몇 명 있어요?**
5. 펫 있어요? **몇 마리 있어요?**

Pattern Practice (몇 개/명/마리 있어요?)

Practice counting native numbers in Korean. Ask your partner how many items/people/animals there are in the pictures. Make sure to use the appropriate counters.

Model Pattern

A: 펜이 몇 개 있어요?

B: 두 개 있어요.

Activity 1: 가방 안에 뭐가 있어요?

Pair up with a classmate, and ask your partner what kind of things they have in their bag and then find out how many there are.

Model Conversation

김유진:	데이빗 씨, 지금 가방 안에 뭐가 있어요?
데이빗:	한국어 **책 한 권**하고 경제학 **책 한 권** 있어요.
	유진 씨는 가방 안에 뭐가 있어요?
김유진:	저는 생물학 책하고 볼펜이 있어요.
데이빗:	볼펜은 **몇 개 있어요?**
김유진:	두 **개** 있어요.

Your Own Conversation

A: _____ 씨, 지금 가방 안에 뭐가 있어요?

B: _____.

_____ 씨는 가방 안에 뭐가 있어요?

A: 저는 _____하고 _____이/가 있어요.

B: _____은 몇 개/권 있어요?

(Ask how many of the things are in the bag.)

A: _____.

Activity 2: 오늘 듣는 수업에 학생이 몇 명 있는지 말해 보세요.

Talk about a class you have today, and find out how many students there are in the class.

Model Conversation

김유진:	에밀리 씨, 오늘 수업 있으세요?
데이빗:	네, 한국어 수업이 있어요.
김유진:	한국어 반에 학생들이 많아요?
데이빗:	네, 많아요.
김유진:	학생이 **몇 명 있어요?**
데이빗:	35 **명** 있어요.

Your Own Conversation

학생 1: _____ 씨, 오늘 수업 있으세요?

학생 2: 네, _____ 수업이 있어요.
                  (Name of the class.)

학생 1: _____ 반에 학생이 많아요?

학생 2: 네/아니요, _____.

학생 1: 학생이 _____?
        (Ask how many students there are in the class.)

학생 2: _____.

Activity 3: 반 친구에게 가지고 있는 물건, 펫, 형제, 룸메이트, 책의 갯수를 물어 보세요.

Interview three classmates for information about the number of their pets, siblings, books, roommates, and so forth they have, and then report it to the class. Take notes of your interview in the table below. Be sure to use the appropriate counters, and then report it to the class.

Interview Questions

1. 가방 안에 책이 몇 **권** 있어요?
2. 볼펜이 몇 **개** 있어요?
3. 형제[17]가 몇 **명** 있어요?
4. 펫 있어요? 몇 **마리** 있어요?
5. 룸메이트 있어요? 몇 **명** 있어요?

	e.g. 에밀리	친구 1:	친구 2:	친구 3:
1. 책	2 권			
2. 볼펜	5 개			
3. 형제	오빠 1 명 & 여동생 1 명			
4. 펫	개 1 마리			
5. 룸메이트	(X)			

---

[17] 형제: brothers and sisters

Model Report

에밀리 씨는 가방 안에 책이 두 권 있어요. 볼펜은 다섯 개 있어요. 형제는 오빠 한
명하고 여동생 한 명 있어요. 펫은 개 한 마리 있어요. 룸메이트는 없어요.

Your Report

_____

_____

_____

_____

_____

Cultural Awareness: Numbers Koreans Like and Dislike 한국인과 숫자

What is a number that Koreans like the most? It is the number 7, which is believed to be lucky, just like in other cultures. What is a number that Koreans dislike the most? It is the number 4, known as "dead 4." The number 4 is called 사 [Sa] in Korean, which has the same pronunciation as the Chinese letter 死 [Sa], meaning "death" in Chinese. Thus, people believe that the number 4 is associated with misfortune.

Koreans like to celebrate the 100th day of some occasions. People throw a big party for the 100th day of a baby's birth, and young people celebrate the 100th-day anniversary of their meeting as a couple. For high school students in Korea, the college entrance exam is the most important occasion for them, and they are determined, once again, to do well on the exam 100 days before the college entrance exam. They exchange some gifts like rice cakes, sticky candy, and cushions, which are believed to bring luck.

Figure 7.1: Numbers.

Credits

Chapter 8. Introducing Your Family

집이 어디예요?

Objectives

- You will be able to ask and answer questions about someone's hometown and family.
- You will be able to introduce your family.
- You will be able to write about your family and your friend's family.

Key Expressions and Structures

- 집/고향이 어디예요?: Where is your hometown?
- 형제 있으세요?: Do you have brothers and sisters?
- 형제가 몇 명 있어요?: How many brothers and sisters do you have?
- 부모님: parents, 가족: family, 형제: brothers and sisters

Task: Introduce Your Family

Talk about your hometown and your family. Introduce your family by saying, for example, where your parents live, how many brothers and sisters you have, where they live, and what they do/study.

Practice Questions

1. 집이 어디예요?
2. 부모님은 어디 계세요?
3. 형제 있으세요? 몇 명 있어요?
4. 동생/언니/오빠/누나/형은 어디 있어요?
5. 동생/언니/오빠/누나/형하고 사이가 어때요?

Activity 1: 집이 어디이고 가족이 몇 명인지 말해 보세요.

Pair up with a classmate, and talk about your families. Ask your partner about their hometown, parents, brothers and sisters, and what they do.

Model Conversation

김유진:	데이빗 씨, **집이 어디예요?**
데이빗:	시카고예요. 부모님하고 동생이 시카고에 있어요.
	유진 씨는 **집이 어디예요?**
김유진:	저는 집이 한국 서울이에요.
데이빗:	부모님이 한국에 계세요?
김유진:	네, 형제들도 한국에 있어요.
데이빗:	형제가 **몇 명이에요?**
김유진:	누나 한 명하고 동생 한 명 있어요.
	누나는 대학교 4 학년이에요. 그리고 동생은 고등학생이에요.
	데이빗 씨도 **형제 있어요?**
데이빗:	네, 저는 형이 한 명 있어요. 형도 대학생이에요.
	생물학을 공부해요.

Your Own Conversation

A: _____ 씨, 집이 어디예요?

B: _____이에요/예요.

_____씨는 _____?

(Where is your hometown?)

A: 저는 집이 _____이에요/예요.

B: 부모님이 _____에 계세요?

(Are your parents living there?)

A: 네/아니요. 형제들도/은 _____에 있어요.

(Say where your brothers and sisters live.)

B: 형제가 _____?

(How many brothers and sisters do you have?)

A: _____._____.

_____.

(Answer how many brothers and sisters you have, what they do/study, their school year, etc.)

_____씨도 _____?

(Do you have brothers and sisters, too?)

B: 네/아니요. 저도/는 _____ 있어요.

_____.

(Answer how many brothers and sisters you have, what they do/study, their school year, etc.)

Activity 2: 가족 사진을 보면서 가족을 소개해 보세요.

Bring a photo of your family, and introduce your family in front of the class.

Figure 8.1: My family photo.

Sample Report

우리 가족이에요. 우리 집은 한국 서울이에요. 아버지하고 어머니가 서울에 계세요. 오빠 가족도 서울에 있어요. 조카[18]가 두 명 있어요. 이름이 현지하고 지윤이에요. 현지는 초등학생이에요. 바이올린[19]을 해요. 지윤이는 두 살이에요. 저는 우리 가족을 사랑해요.

Your Report

_____

_____

_____

_____

_____

Activity 3: 친구 가족에 대해서 써 보세요.

Interview your classmate about their home and family, and write about their family. Take notes of your interview in the table below and then report it to the class.

Interview Questions

1. _____ 씨는 집이 어디예요?
2. 부모님은 어디 계세요?
3. 형제 있으세요?/형제가 몇 명이에요?
4. 동생/언니/오빠/누나/형은 어디 있어요?
5. (동생/언니/오빠/누나/형은) 몇 살이에요?/학생이에요?/전공이 뭐예요?

---

[18] 조카: nephew/niece
[19] 바이올린: violin

이름	집	가족
e.g.: 에밀리	시카고	부모님: 아버지하고 어머니, 시카고 언니: 1 명, 뉴욕, 대학원생, 생물학 동생: 1 명, 시카고, 초등학생
친구:_____		

Model Writing

에밀리 씨는 집이 시카고예요. 부모님이 시카고에 계세요. 형제는 언니 한 명하고 동생 한 명 있어요. 에밀리 씨 언니는 뉴욕에 있어요. 대학원생이에요. 생물학을 전공해요. 동생이 한 명 있어요. 초등학생이에요. 동생은 시카고에서 부모님하고 같이 살아요.

Your Report

_____

_____

_____

_____

_____

_____

Cultural Awareness: Family Terms 가족 호칭

Korean family terms are gender-specific, depending on whether you are male or female. If you are male, then you'd have 형 (older brother) and 누나 (older sister). If you are a female, then you'd have 오빠 (older brother) and 언니 (older sister). For younger siblings, you call them by their names just like in Western culture.

Another interesting thing about Korean family terms is that they are not just used for family but they are extended to people to whom you are close. That's why you often hear girls call a guy 오빠 in Korean drama. Even though they are not related by blood, they tend to use family terms to address people close to them. In Korea, you can use 어머니/아버지, not just to your parents but to your friends' parents. Your friends' parents are people close to you, and you'd like to be nice to them, so in Korea, people treat their friends' parents as their own. Thus, you never should address them by their names in Korea. You can also hear people use a family term at a restaurant to call a waiter/waitress. For example, people use a term 이모 (aunt) for a middle-aged female server and 언니 (older sister) for a young female server. When ordering at a Korean restaurant, try saying "이모, 비빔밥 하나 주세요!" ("One bibimbap please!").

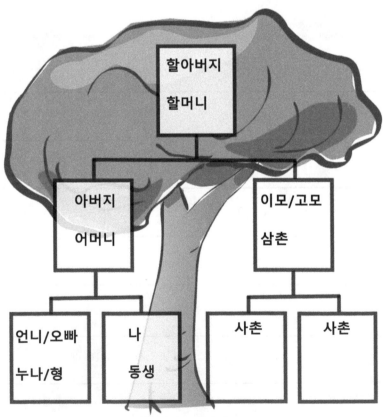

Figure 8.2: Family tree.

Credit

- Fig. 8.2: Source: https://pixabay.com/photo-297812/.

Chapter 9. Describing Your Class Schedule

한국어 수업이 언제 있어요?

Objectives

- You will be able to tell time in Korean.
- You will be able to describe your daily and weekly schedule.
- You will be able to ask to check someone's schedule and set up a meeting at a specific time.
- You will be able to talk about what courses you take and your class schedule.

Key Expressions and Structures

- 몇 시에 V-해요?: What time do you do V?
- N 수업이 언제 있어요?: When do you have N class?
- 이번 학기에 몇 과목 들어요?: How many courses are you taking this semester?
- 오전/오후/저녁에 뭐 해요?: What do you do in the morning/afternoon/evening?
- Days: 일요일(Sunday), 월요일(Monday), 화요일(Tuesday), 수요일(Wednesday), 목요일(Thursday), 금요일(Friday), 토요일(Saturday)

Task: Describe Your Daily and Class Schedule

Describe your daily and class schedule. Check out a friend's schedule, and set up a meeting at a specific time.

Practice Questions

1. 보통 **몇 시에** 일어나요?
2. 보통 **몇 시에** 자요?
3. **이번 학기에 몇 과목 들어요?**
4. **몇 시에** 수업이 있어요?
5. 한국어 수업이 **언제 있어요?**

Pattern Practice (Telling Time: 몇 시 몇 분)

Practice telling time in Korean. Say daily activities with a specific time—for example: 오전 일곱시에 일어나요. 여덟시에 학교에 가요. First, draw hands of clock in the pictures and then say what time you do the activities.

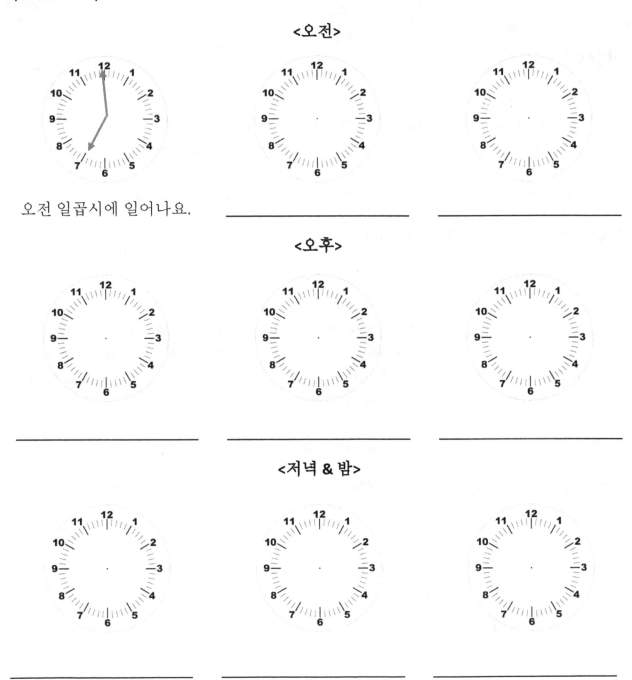

\<오전\>

오전 일곱시에 일어나요. _____ _____

\<오후\>

_____ _____ _____

\<저녁 & 밤\>

_____ _____ _____

Activity 1: 오늘 스케줄을 물어 보고 파트너와 같이 한 가지 오늘 할 계획을 짜 보세요.

Pair up with a classmate, and choose one day that you/your partner have a class in the morning and no class in the afternoon. Ask each other about your schedule for the day and make plans together for the afternoon. Be sure to say a specific time when making plans.

Model Conversation

김유진:	데이빗씨, 오늘 수업 있으세요?
데이빗:	네, 한국어 수업이 있어요.
김유진:	**몇 시에 있어요?**
데이빗:	오전 10 시 30 분에 있어요.
김유진:	오후에도 수업이 있어요?
데이빗:	아니요, 금요일 오후에는 수업이 없어요.
김유진:	그럼, 저하고 같이 쇼핑하러 백화점에 가요.
데이빗:	네, 좋아요. **몇 시에 가요?**
김유진:	3 시 어때요?
데이빗:	네, 좋아요.
김유진:	그럼, 3 시에 백화점 앞에서 만나요.

Your Own Conversation

A: _____ 씨, 오늘 수업 있으세요?

B: 네, _____ 수업이 있어요.

A: _____?

(What time do you have the class?)

B: _____에 있어요.

A: _____?

(Do you have a class in the afternoon, too?)

B: 아니요, _____ 오후에는 수업이 없어요.

                (Say what day it is today.)

A: 그럼, 저하고 같이 _____.

                (Suggest doing something together.)

B: 네, 좋아요. _____?

                (What time do we meet?)

A: _____?

      (Suggest a time to meet.)

B: 네, 좋아요.

A: 그럼, _____.

                (Let's meet up at that time!)

Activity 2: 이번 학기 듣는 수업과 시간표를 물어 보세요.

Ask your partner about their class schedule this semester. Complete the class schedule in the table.

Model Conversation

	시간 (time)	월요일	화요일	수요일	목요일	금요일
오전	10 시 10 분	수학		수학		수학
	11 시 15 분	한국어	한국어	한국어	한국어	한국어
오후	1 시 25 분		경제학		경제학	
	3 시 30 분	피아노		피아노		피아노

김유진: 데이빗 씨, 이번 학기에 수업 **몇 과목 들어요?**

데이빗: 4 과목 들어요. 한국어, 경제학, 수학, 피아노 수업을 들어요.

김유진: 한국어 수업은 **언제 있어요?**

데이빗: 매일 11 시 15 분에 있어요.

김유진: 수학 수업은 **언제 있어요?**

데이빗: 월요일, 수요일, 금요일 오전 10 시 10 분에 있어요.

김유진: 경제학 수업은 **언제 있어요?**

데이빗: 화요일하고 목요일 1 시 25 분에 있어요.

김유진: 피아노 수업은 **언제 있어요?**

데이빗: 월요일, 수요일, 금요일 오후 3 시 30 분에 있어요.

Your Partner's Schedule

	시간(time)	월요일	화요일	수요일	목요일	금요일
오전						
오후						

A: _____ 씨, 이번 학기에 수업 몇 과목 들어요?

B: _____과목 들어요. _____을 들어요.

(Say the titles of the courses.)

A: _____ 수업은 언제 있어요?

(Say course #1.)

B: _____에 있어요.

A: _____ 수업은 언제 있어요?

(Say course #2.)

B: _____에 있어요.

A: _____ 수업은 언제 있어요?

(Say course #3.)

B: _____에 있어요.

(You can repeat the question if you take more courses.)

Activity 3: 반 친구의 하루 일과에 대해서 물어 보고 일과표를 완성해 보세요.

Interview a classmate about their daily schedule, and complete the schedule below. Be sure to include the specific time and the location of the activities.

Interview Questions

1. 몇 시에 일어나요?
2. 몇 시에 학교에 가요?
3. 몇 시에 수업 들어요?
4. 몇 시에 점심 먹어요?

5. 몇 시에 숙제해요?
6. 몇 시에 집에 가요?
7. 몇 시에 저녁 먹어요?
8. 몇 시에 자요?

Sample Schedule

	Time	**Activities**
오전	7 시 30 분	일어나요.
	9 시	학교에 가요.
	10 시 10 분	SGIS 빌딩에서 한국어 수업을 들어요.
오후	12 시 30 분	학교 식당에서 점심을 먹어요.
	1 시 25 분	경제학 수업을 들어요.
	4 시	도서관에서 숙제 해요.
저녁	6 시	집에 가요
	7 시	기숙사 식당에서 저녁을 먹어요.
밤	11 시 30 분	자요.

_____'s Schedule

	Time	Activities
오전		
오후		
저녁		
밤		

Activity 4: 여러분의 하루 일과를 써 보세요.

Write about your daily schedule from morning to night.

Model Writing

저는 보통 아침 7 시에 일어나요. 7 시 반에 아침을 먹어요. 그리고 8 시에 체육관에서 운동해요. 오전 10 시 10 분에 한국어 수업이 있어요. 그래서 9 시 50 분에 학교에 가요. 12 시 반에 학교 식당에서 점심을 먹어요. 오후에도 수업이 있어요. 화요일하고 목요일 2 시에 경제학 수업을 들어요. 월요일, 수요일, 금요일 3 시 20 분에는 피아노 수업이 있어요. 보통 저녁 6 시에 기숙사에 와요. 저녁 7 시에 기숙사 식당에서 저녁을 먹어요. 8 시에 방에서 숙제를 해요. 보통 밤 11 시 반에 자요.

Your Report

_____

_____

_____

_____

_____

_____

Cultural Awareness: Night Culture in Korea 한국의 밤 문화

A number of shops and restaurants are open late in Korea regardless of the types of items/foods that are sold in them. And most of the convenience stores are open 24 hours in Korea. Due to the lights from the shops/restaurants that are open late, you'd feel pretty safe even when walking alone on the street at night. The reason why a lot of stores are open late is that people like to go out with friends; Koreans think that relationships with others are important. They really enjoy hanging out with people and often get together with friends and colleagues. There is a special term for the gathering with colleagues: 회식. On the gathering day, people meet to have dinner together first, and then they go have a drink for the second round. Going on a second and even a third round is very common. Usually, they go to karaoke on the third round. There are famous places where you can enjoy the night culture in Korea: 홍대, 강남 in Seoul. If you ever have a chance to go to Korea, go to those areas and enjoy the night culture of Korea. You'll be amazed!

Figure 9.1: A street at night in Korea.

Credits

- IMG 9.1a: Source: https://pixabay.com/images/id-42809/.
- IMG 9.1b: Source: https://pixabay.com/images/id-42809/.
- IMG 9.1c: Source: https://pixabay.com/images/id-42809/.
- IMG 9.1d: Source: https://pixabay.com/images/id-42809/.
- IMG 9.1e: Source: https://pixabay.com/images/id-42809/.
- IMG 9.1f: Source: https://pixabay.com/images/id-42809/.
- IMG 9.1g: Source: https://pixabay.com/images/id-42809/.
- IMG 9.1h: Source: https://pixabay.com/images/id-42809/.
- IMG 9.1i: Source: https://pixabay.com/images/id-42809/.
- Fig. 9.1: Source: https://pixabay.com/en/nightlife-republic-of-korea-jongno-2162772/.

Chapter 10. Talking about Your Past

초등학생이었어요.

Objectives

- You will be able to say what you did in the past.
- You will be able to describe the activities you did on the weekend.
- You will be able to describe what you did at a specific time for one day.
- You will be able to compare what you were to what you are in the present.

Key Expressions and Structures

- V/A -었/았/ㅆ어요: past tense
- [Past time/day]에 뭐 했어요?: What did you do in/on/at [past time/day]?
- 주말에 뭐 했어요?: What did you do on the weekend?
- 어땠어요?: How was it?
- 초등학생이었어요: I was an elementary student.
- 어제: yesterday, 지난: last, 작년: last year, 10년 전: 10 years ago

Task: Talking about Your Past

Talk about what you did in the past, and describe what has changed now compared to your past.

Practice Questions

1. **지난** 주말에 **뭐 했어요**?
2. **작년** 생일에 **뭐 했어요**?
3. **어제** 몇 시에 한국어 수업이 **있었어요**?
4. **어제** 어디에서 점심 **먹었어요**?
5. **어제** 몇 시에 **잤어요**?

Pattern Practice (Past Tense: V/A 어제 뭐 했어요?)

Suppose that yesterday you did the activities shown in the pictures. Describe what you did yesterday. Make sure to use the past tense ~었/았/ㅆ어요.

일곱시에 일어났어요.

_____

_____

_____

_____

_____

_____

_____

_____

Activity 1: 지난 주말에 한 일을 말해 보세요.

Ask your partner about what they did on the weekend. Include some follow-up questions, such as who they did the activity with, why they did it, and how it was.

Model Conversation

데이빗:	유진 씨, **주말에 뭐 했어요?**
김유진:	도서관에서 숙제 했어요.
데이빗:	숙제가 **많았어요?**
김유진:	네, 한국어 숙제하고 경제학 숙제 했어요.
	데이빗 씨는 **주말에 뭐 했어요?**
데이빗:	저는 친구 생일 파티에 갔어요.
	지난 토요일이 제 친구 민지 생일이었어요.
김유진:	아, 그래요? 파티는 **재미있었어요?**
데이빗:	네, 한국어 반 친구들이 파티에 많이 왔어요.
김유진:	네, 파티에서 **뭐 했어요?**
데이빗:	같이 음악 들었어요. 친구들이 한국 음악을 좋아해요.
김유진:	아, 그래요? 저도 한국 음악을 좋아해요.

Your Own Conversation

A: _____ 씨, 주말에 뭐 했어요?

B: _____

A: 아, 그래요? 누구하고 같이 _____?

(Who did you do it with?)

B: _____.

A: _____?

(How was it? Was it fun?)

B: _____.

_____ 씨는 주말에 뭐 했어요?

A: 저는 _____.

B: 아, 그래요? 누구하고 같이 _____?

(Who did you do it with?)

A: _____.

B: _____?

(How was it? Was it fun?)

A: _____.

Activity 2: 10 년 전과 지금의 나를 비교해 보세요.

Think about yourself as compared to 10 years ago. What has changed since then? Take note of it in the table below, and report it to the class.

Sample Notes

	2010 년에는 ...	지금은 ...
School	초등학생	대학생
Place you live(d) in	한국 서울	미국 블루밍턴
Foods you like(d)	피자, 햄버거	비빔밥, 불고기
Things you didn't/couldn't do 10 years ago but you do/can do now	• 수영을 잘 못 했어요. 그런데 지금은 아주 잘 해요. • 한국 음악을 안 들었어요. 그런데 지금은 자주 들어요.	

Model Report

저는 2010 년에 초등학생이었어요. 그런데 지금은 대학생이에요. 2010 년에는 한국 서울에서 살았어요. 그런데 지금은 미국 블루밍턴에서 살아요. 피자하고 햄버거를 좋아했어요. 그런데 지금은 비빔밥하고 불고기를 좋아해요. 수영을 잘 못 했어요. 그런데 지금은 아주 잘 해요. 2010 년에는 한국 음악을 안 들었어요. 그런데 지금은 자주 들어요.

Your Notes

	_____년에는 ...	지금은 ...
School		
Place you live(d) in		
Foods you like(d)		
Things you didn't/couldn't do 10 years ago but you do/can do now		

Your Report

_____

_____

_____

_____

_____

_____

Activity 3: 기억에 남는 여행에 대해서 말해 보세요.

Tell us about your travel experience. Choose one memorable trip you went on in the past and describe what you did on the trip. Interview your classmate and learn about their memorable trip. You may ask questions below. Take notes of it in the table, and report it to the class.

Yujin's Memorable Trip

Interview Questions	Notes
1. 어디에 갔어요?	엘에이 디즈니랜드
2. 누구하고 갔어요?	언니하고 같이 갔어요.
3. 언제 갔어요?	2018 년 여름 방학에 갔어요.
4. 뭐 했어요?	롤러코스터, 미키 마우스, 미니 마우스, 백설 공주 (snow white), 퍼레이드
5. 뭐 먹었어요? 맛있었어요?	햄버거, 추로스 (churros)
6. 어디에서 잤어요?	디즈니 호텔
7. 재미있었어요?	네

Model Report

유진 씨는 2018 년 여름 방학에 디즈니랜드에 갔어요. 언니하고 같이 갔어요. 롤러코스터를 탔어요. 그리고 미키 마우스하고 미니 마우스하고 사진을 찍었어요. 미키와 미니 마우스는 아주 친절했어요. 백설 공주도 만났어요. 아주 예뻤어요. 점심에 저는 햄버거를 먹었어요. 언니는 피자를 먹었어요. 그리고 아이스크림하고 추로스도 먹었어요. 저녁에는 퍼레이드를 봤어요. 그리고 저녁 9 시에 호텔에 갔어요. 참 재미있었어요.

_____'s Memorable Trip

Interview Questions	Notes
1. 어디에 갔어요?	
2. 누구하고 갔어요?	
3. 언제 갔어요?	
4. 뭐 했어요?	
5. 뭐 먹었어요? 맛있었어요?	
6. 어디에서 잤어요?	
7. 재미있었어요?	

Your Report

_____

_____

_____

_____

_____

Cultural Awareness: Celebrating Birthdays in Korea 생일 축하

There are several special ways of celebrating one's birthday in Korea. The most important thing to do on someone's birthday is to make seaweed soup for the birthday person. Traditionally, mothers prepare the seaweed soup (미역국) in the morning. People even make sure that the birthday person ate 미역국 on the day. Where did the tradition come from, then? Seaweed is known to be good for new mothers in helping with recovery. Korean women eat a lot of seaweed soup after giving birth to a child. That's how this tradition started.

In Korea, there are two special birthdays that people celebrate: one is 돌, the first birthday, and the other is 환갑, the sixtieth birthday. For 돌, parents invite many people and throw a big birthday party for their baby, as shown in the picture below. People bring some special gifts to celebrate the baby's first birthday. The common gifts for 돌 are a gold ring and money. For 환갑, children throw a birthday party for their parent. As a gift, they send their parent on a trip; some families prepare an appreciation plaque for them.

Young people usually gather at a café to celebrate a friend's birthday. They usually give a birthday present to the birthday person and eat cake together. In return, the birthday person treats the friends to dinner, which is certainly different than American birthday customs.

Figure 10.1: The first birthday party 돌잔치.

Credits

Chapter 11. Talking about Things You Didn't Do

어제 파티에 못 갔어요.

Objectives

- You will be able to make negative sentences.
- You will be able to say what you didn't do in the past.
- You will be able to make a difference between two negative forms depending on a situation.
- You will be able to talk about which activities you are good and not good at.

Key Expressions and Structures

- 안 V/A -어/아요: do not
- 못 V/A -어/아요: cannot
- 잘해요: to be good at something
- 잘 못해요: to be not good at something
- 몰라요: I don't know

Task: Talking about What You Didn't Do

Ask about what your partner probably couldn't do yesterday and ask why.

Practice Questions

1. 어제 도서관에 갔어요?

2. 선생님 전화번호 알아요?

3. 매일 엄마하고 전화해요?

4. 매일 아침 먹어요?

5. 노래 잘 해요?

Activity 1: 친구들이 어제 하지 않은 일들을 알아내 보세요.

Ask your classmates about what they did yesterday until you find what they didn't do. (You can make up and ask as many questions as you want.) Make sure to use the negative form 안 to say what they didn't do. Ask three classmates and take notes in the table and report it to the class.

Model Conversation

데이빗:	유진 씨, 어제 한국어 수업 들었어요?
김유진:	네, 들었어요.
데이빗:	그럼 도서관에 갔어요?
김유진:	네, 갔어요.
데이빗:	친구도 만났어요?
김유진:	네, 만났어요.
데이빗:	그럼 방 청소 했어요?
김유진:	아니요, **안** 했어요.

이름	Things They Did	Things They Didn't Do
e.g.유진	한국어 수업, 도서관, 친구	방 청소
친구 1.		
친구 2.		
친구 3.		

Model Report

유진 씨는 어제 한국어 수업을 들었어요. 그리고 도서관에 갔어요. 그리고 친구도 만났어요. 그런데 방 청소는 안했어요.

Your Report

_____

_____

_____

_____

_____

_____

Activity 2: 지난 주말에 하지 못한 일들에 대해서 말해 보세요.

Ask your partner what they couldn't do yesterday because of some situation. Ask about what your partner probably couldn't do yesterday and ask why. Make sure to use the negative form 못 when you didn't do it because of an outside cause, not because of your intention.

Model Conversation

데이빗:	유진 씨, 어제 에밀리 씨 생일 파티에 갔어요?
김유진:	아니요, **못** 갔어요.
데이빗:	왜 **못** 갔어요?
김유진:	시험이 있었어요. 그래서 바빴어요.
	데이빗 씨는 파티에 갔어요?
데이빗:	아니요, 저도 **못** 갔어요.
김유진:	왜요?
데이빗:	숙제가 많았어요. 그래서 **못** 갔어요.

Your Own Conversation

A: _____ 씨, 어제 _____?

                                            (Ask if B did something yesterday.)

B: 아니요, _____.

A: _____?

    (Ask why.)

B: _____.

    _____씨는 _____?

    (Ask the same question to A.)

A: 네/아니요. _____.

B: _____

    (If the answer is no, then ask why.)

A: _____

Activity 3: 우리 반에서 누가 수학을 잘해요?

Find someone who is good at the following activities: 요리, 중국어, 수학, 수영, 농구, 노래, 피아노, 바이올린, for example. Move around and ask your classmates. Write their names in the table and report to the class. Make sure to use the expression 잘 해요 when someone is good at something and 잘 못해요 when not.

Sample Interview

A:	유진 씨, 수학 **잘 해요**?
B:	아니요, **잘 못해요.**
A:	그럼, 중국어 **잘 해요**?
B:	네, **잘 해요.**

Activities	이름
중국어	유진
수학	
수영	
농구	데이빗
노래	
피아노	
바이올린	

Cultural Awareness: College Entrance Exam in Korea 수능 시험

Koreans place a high value on education. Perhaps entering a prestigious university is everyone's top priority in Korea. The college entrance exam in Korea is called "수능," which is similar to the SAT in the United States. It is regarded as a nationwide annual event. On the day of the college entrance exam, people working for public offices or private companies with more than 20 employees go to work one hour later than usual in order not to cause traffic jams during rush hour so that students will not be late for the exam on the day. Also, the takeoff and the landing of airplanes is prohibited between 1:10 p.m. and 1:35 p.m. when the listening part of a foreign language area is taken.

Korean parents' passion for their childeren's education is well known. You will see many parents praying for good luck for their childern in front of a school gate on the exam day. And high school freshmen and juniors are also busy cheering for their school's senior students on the day. They wait for the seniors in front of the school gate in order to give gifts wishing for good luck. The gifts given to the senior on the day are 찹살떡 (sticky rice cake) and 엿 (sticky caramel). The reason why people give 찹살떡 and 엿 as gifts is that the word "passing (a test)" is (시험에) 붙다, which literally means "stick to a test" in Korean. The tradition of giving 찹쌀떡 and 엿 as gifts on the exam day came from this.

One more important thing that you should know about 수능 is that students will never eat 미역국 (seaweed soup) on the exam day. It is a superstition, but everyone in Korean believes in this superstition. The reason why students don't eat 미역국 is that the slippery texture of seaweed gives the idea of failing. Actually, "failing a test" in Korean is 미끌어지다, which literally means "slip a test." The superstition originated from this idea. So, you should be careful of many things on the day of the college entrance exam in Korea.

Figure 11.1: University.

Credit

- Fig. 11.1: Source: https://pixabay.com/images/id-3588192/.

Chapter 12. Talking about Your Preferences

어느 식당이 맛있어요?

Objectives

- You will be able to talk about what kind of food you like and which restaurant you go to often.
- You will be able to find out someone's preference for food, music, sports, movies, and so forth.
- You will be able to conduct a survey of classmates' favorite places in the city where they live, such as a mall, a coffee shop, a restaurant, a market, a bank, or a clothing/shoe store.

Key Expressions and Structures

- 무슨 N(을/를) 좋아해요?: What kind of N do you like?
- 어느 [place]에 자주 가세요?: Which place do you often go?
- V-(으)러 [place]에 가요.: Go to the [place] to do V.
- 한국 음식: 김치찌개 (kimchi stew), 순두부 찌개 (tofu soup), 비빔밥 (bibimbop)

Task: Talking about Your Favorite Places

Take a survey to find out your classmates' preferences for food, music, sports, and movies, and find out their favorite places to go in the city.

Practice Questions

1. **무슨** 음식을 좋아하세요?

2. **어느** 한국 식당이 맛있어요?

3. 장 **보러** 어느 마켓에 자주 **가세요**?

4. 영화 **보러** 어느 극장에 자주 **가세요**?

Activity 1: 좋아하는 음식과 맛있는 식당에 대해서 말해 보세요.

Talk about what kind of food you like and which restaurant you go to often. At the end of your talk, suggest that your partner might want to try it, too.

Model Conversation

데이빗:	에밀리 씨는 **무슨** 음식을 좋아하세요?
에밀리:	저는 한국 음식을 좋아해요.
데이빗:	**어느** 한국 식당이 맛있어요?
김유진:	저는 학교 앞 '이모 식당'에 자주 가요.
	비빔밥하고 김치 찌개가 맛있어요.
데이빗:	아, 그래요? 순두부 찌개도 맛있어요?
김유진:	네, 괜찮아요. 에밀리 씨, 순두부 찌개 좋아하세요?
데이빗:	네, 아주 좋아해요.
김유진:	그럼, 오늘 점심 **먹으러** '이모 식당'에 같이 가요!
데이빗:	네, 좋아요.
김유진:	그럼, 한국어 수업 끝나고 가요!

Your Own Conversation

A: ＿＿＿＿＿＿＿＿ 씨는 무슨 음식을 좋아하세요?

B: 저는 ＿＿＿＿＿＿ 음식을 좋아해요.

A: 어느 ＿＿＿＿＿＿ 식당이 맛있어요?

(Which restaurant food is tasty around here?)

B: 저는 ＿＿＿＿＿＿＿＿＿＿에 자주 가요.

＿＿＿＿＿＿＿＿＿＿ 이/가 맛있어요.

(Dish A and Dish B.)

A: 아, 그래요? ＿＿＿＿＿＿＿＿ 도 맛있어요?

(Dish C.)

B: 네/아니요. _____씨, _____ 좋아하세요?

                              (Dish C.)

A: 네, 아주 좋아해요.

B: 그럼, _____

                    (Suggest going to the restaurant to have lunch today.)

A: 네, 좋아요.

B: 그럼, 한국어 수업 끝나고 가요!

Activity 2: 반 친구들이 좋아하는 음식, 음악, 운동, 영화에 대해서 알아 보고 표를 완성해 보세요.

Take a survey to find out your classmates' preferences for food, music, sports, movies, and so forth. Take notes in the table below, and share the results at the end.

Survey Questions

1. Interview two classmates about what kinds of food, music, sports, and movies they like, as in Example 1.

   o 음식: 한국 음식, 중국 음식, 일본 음식, 미국 음식, 멕시칸 음식(Mexican food), etc.

   o 음악: 클래식 (classical music), 팝 (pop), 록 (rock), 발라드 (ballad), 힙합 (hip-hop), 재즈 (jazz), 이디엠 (electronic dance music), etc.

   o 영화: 코미디 (comedy), 액션 (action), 드라마 (drama), 로맨스 (romance), 공포 (thriller), 공상 과학 (science fiction), 만화 영화 (animation), etc.

   o 운동: 농구 (basketball), 야구 (baseball), 축구 (soccer), 미식 축구 (American football), 테니스, 골프, 수영, etc.

Example 1.	데이빗: 에밀리 씨, 무슨 <u>음식</u> 좋아해요?
	에밀리: 저는 <u>한국 음식</u> 좋아해요.

2. Survey of your classmates' preference for specific items, as in Example 2.

    o   김치 찌개 **vs.** 순두부 찌개

    o   딸기[20] 아이스크림 **vs.** 초콜릿 아이스크림

    o   Exo **vs.** BTS

    o   스파이더맨 **vs.** 앤트맨

Example 2.	데이빗: 유진 씨는 **어느** <u>찌개</u>가 맛있어요?
	김유진: 저는 <u>순두부 찌개</u>가 맛있어요.

	e.g. 에밀리	친구 1.	친구 2.
음식	한국 음식		
음악	재즈		
영화	로맨스 영화		
운동	수영		
김치 찌개 vs. 순두부 찌개	순두부 찌개		
딸기 아이스크림 vs. 초콜릿아이스크림	딸기 아이스크림		
Exo vs. BTS	BTS		
스파이더맨 vs. 배트맨	스파이더맨		

[20] 딸기: strawberry

Activity 3: 여러분이 사는 도시에서 자주 가는 장소에 대해서 알아 보세요.

Interview two classmates, and find out their favorite places in your city, such as a mall, a coffee shop, a restaurant, a market, a bank, and a clothing/shoe store, as in Example 3.

| Example 3. | 데이빗: 에밀리 씨, **어느** 마켓에 자주 가세요? |
| | 에밀리: 저는 크로거 마켓에 자주 가요. |

	e.g. 에밀리	**친구 1.**	**친구 2.**
마켓	크로거 마켓		
쇼핑 몰	칼리지 몰		
커피숍	스타벅스		
식당	이모 식당		
옷/신발 가게	H&M		
은행	IU Credit Union		

Cultural Awareness: Korean Food 한국 음식

A basic table setting for a Korean meal consists of 밥 (rice), 국 (soup), and 반찬 (side dishes). A rice bowl and a soup bowl are usually placed side by side in the middle of the table. A spoon and a pair of chopsticks are placed to the right of the soup bowl. Typically, Koreans use the spoon for rice and soup and the chopsticks for side dishes.

The side dishes, called 반찬, can include many different kinds of dishes, such as 김치, 나물, 콩자반, and 멸치. Korean meals sometimes may not have a main dish but only side dishes. People often eat side dishes with only rice at home. It is common at a Korean restaurant that side dishes are served before a main dish, as shown in the picture below. People sometimes choose the restaurant just because delicious side dishes are served there. I hope you enjoy many different kinds of side dishes with your main dish when you go to a Korean restaurant.

Figure 12.1: 반찬, side dishes served at a Korean restaurant.

Credit

Chapter 13. Setting Up a Meeting Place

블루밍턴 공원까지 어떻게 가요?

Objectives

- You will be able to say how to get to a place using transportation.
- You will be able to say how long it takes to get to the place.
- You will be able to set up a meeting with someone by saying what time and where to meet.
- You will be able to talk about your favorite trip by saying where, when, with whom you went, how you went, and how long it took, for example.

Key Expressions and Structures

- N 까지 어떻게 가요?: How do you go to N?
- A 에서 B 까지 얼마나 걸려요?: How long does it take to get from A to B?
- N (으)로: by transportation N
- 자전거/차/버스/지하철/비행기로: by bicycle/car/bus/subway/plane
- 걸어서: on foot

Task: Setting Up a Gathering with Your Friends

Set up a gathering with your friends for this coming weekend. Ask your friends if they are available and suggest going to an interesting event for the weekend. Set up a specific time and a place to meet, and explain how to get to the location for the event.

Practice Questions

1. 어디에 살아요?
2. 학교에 **어떻게 가요**?
3. 집**에서** 학교**까지 얼마나 걸려요**?
4. 이번 주말에 시간 있으세요?
5. 저하고 같이 콘서트 보러 가요!

Pattern Practice 1 (집에서 학교까지 어떻게 가요?)

Practice with your partner based on the information provided in the table.

Model Pattern

A: 집**에서** 학교**까지 어떻게 가요**?

B: <u>버스로</u> <u>20 분</u>쯤 걸려요.

Transportation	Duration
버스	20 분
지하철	25 분
걸어서	5 분
자전거	10 분

Pattern Practice 2 (얼마나 걸려요?)

Practice with your partner based on the information provided in the table.

Model Pattern

A: _____에서 _____까지 얼마나 걸려요?

B: _____.

From	To	Transportation	Duration
집	백화점	버스	20 분
한국어 교실	학교 식당	걸어서	5 분
한국	미국	비행기	13 시간
블루밍턴	시카고	차	5 시간

Activity 1: 집에서 학교까지 어떻게 가는지 말해 보세요.

Have a conversation about how to go to school, what kind of transportation to use, and how long it takes.

Model Conversation

데이빗:	유진 씨, 어디 살아요?
김유진:	학교 근처[21] 아파트에 살아요.
데이빗:	**학교까지 어떻게 가요?**
김유진:	보통 **버스로** 가요.
데이빗:	**집에서 학교까지 얼마나 걸려요?**
김유진:	버스로 10 분쯤 **걸려요.**
	데이빗 씨는 어디 살아요?
데이빗:	저는 학교 기숙사에 살아요.
김유진:	**학교까지 얼마나 걸려요?**
데이빗:	보통 **걸어서** 5 분쯤 **걸려요.**

Your Own Conversation

A: _____ 씨, 어디 살아요?

B: _____.

A: 학교까지 어떻게 가요?

B: 보통 _____.

A: _____?

(How long does it take to go from home to school?)

B: _____.

_____ 씨는 어디 살아요?

A: 저는 _____.

---

[21] 근처: around

B: _____?

(How long does it take to go from home to school?)

A: _____.

Activity 2: 여러분이 여행한 곳에 대해서 말해 보세요.

Talk about a good place/city/country where you've traveled. Include information about who you went there with, what you did, how you got there, how long it took, and so forth. Report on the trip to the class. Then, interview two other classmates about their trips. Take notes of what they say in the table.

Interview Questions

1. 어디에 여행 했어요?
2. 언제 갔어요?
3. 누구하고 갔어요?
4. 어떻게 갔어요? 얼마나 걸렸어요?
5. 뭐 했어요?
6. 어땠어요?

Interview Qs.	e.g. 나	나	친구 1.	친구 2.
1.	엘에이			
2.	2018 년 여름 방학			
3.	동생			

4.	비행기 5 시간			
5.	디즈니랜드, 미키 마우스, 백설 공주, etc.			
6.	재미있었어요			

Sample Report

저는 2018 년 여름 방학에 엘에이에 여행 갔어요. 동생하고 같이 갔어요. 인디애나에서 엘에이까지 비행기로 5 시간쯤 걸렸어요. 엘에이는 날씨가 참 좋았어요. 디즈니랜드에 갔어요. 사람들이 참 많았어요. 미키 마우스하고 백설 공주 (snow white) 도 봤어요. 정말 재미있었어요.

Your Report

_____

_____

_____

_____

_____

Activity 3: 이번 주말에 있는 재미있는 행사에 친구하고 같이 가는 약속을 해 보세요.

Set up a gathering with friends to go to an interesting event this coming weekend, such as a sports game, a musical concert, a festival, or a fair. You may choose one of the following events:

Information about Weekend Events

Event	Date	Time	Place	Transportation
농구 경기	10 월 25 일 (토)	7:00 p.m.– 8:30 p.m.	학교 농구장	Bus No. 2 (5 min.)
Monroe County Fair	10 월 26 일 (일)	11:00 a.m.– 5:00 p.m.	문화광장 (Cultural Plaza)	Bus No. 75 (20 min.)
Jazz 공연	11 월 3 일 (토)	5:00 p.m.– 6:00 p.m.	블루밍턴 공원	Bus No. 125 (15 min.)
BTS 콘서트	11 월 4 일 (일)	3:30 p.m.– 5:00 p.m.	아트홀 (Art Hall)	on foot (10 min.)

Model Conversation

데이빗: 제임스 씨, 이번 금요일에 시간 있으세요?

제임스: 네, 괜찮아요. 왜요?

데이빗: 저녁에 학교 농구장에서 경기가 있어요.

제임스: 아, 그래요? 몇 시에 해요?

데이빗: 저녁 7 시에 시작해요. 저하고 같이 농구 보러 가요.

제임스: 네, 좋아요. 그런데 농구장**까지 어떻게 가요?**

데이빗: 기숙사 앞에서 2 번 버스를 타요.

제임스: **얼마나 걸려요?**

데이빗: 버스로 5 분쯤 걸려요.

제임스: 그럼, 금요일에 봐요.

Your Own Conversation

A: _____ 씨, 이번 _____에 시간 있으세요?

B: 네, 괜찮아요. 왜요?

A: _____

(Say there is an interesting event on the day.)

B: 아, 그래요? 몇 시에 해요?

A: _____에 시작해요. _____

(time)　　　　　　　　(Suggest going to the event together.)

B: 네, 좋아요. 그런데 _____?

(How do I go to the event place?)

A: _____.

B: _____?

(How long does it take to get there?)

A: _____

B: 그럼, _____.

(Let's meet up on the day!)

Activity 4: 지난 주말에 행사 (Activity 3) 를 갔다고 생각하고 지난 주말에 대해 글을 써 보세요.

Suppose that you went to an event (Activity 3) last weekend; write about your last weekend.

Model Writing

지난 토요일에 블루밍턴 공원에서 재즈 콘서트가 있었어요. 저는 한국어 반 친구들하고 같이 콘서트를 보러 갔어요. 공원까지 125 번 버스를 탔어요. 15 분쯤 걸렸어요. 공원에는 사람들이 아주 많았어요. 콘서트는 5 시부터 6 시까지 했어요. 날씨도 좋고 재즈 음악도 정말 아름다웠어요. 콘서트가 끝나고 친구들하고 커피숍에 갔어요. 오래간만에 친구들하고 커피도 마시고 이야기도 많이 했어요. 지난 주말은 정말 재미있었어요.

Your Writing

_____

_____

_____

_____

_____

_____

Cultural Awareness: Four Seasons in Korea 한국의 사계절

There are four distinct seasons in Korea: spring, summer, autumn, and winter. Korea is located in the East Asian monsoon belt. The mean temperature of the hottest month (August) is above 25°C (approximately 77°F). The mean temperature during winter is generally below zero. The mean temperature in January in Seoul is -3.5°C (approximately 30°F).

The summer monsoon season, called 장마, "the rainy spell," brings abundant moisture from the ocean and produces heavy rainfalls. About 70 percent of Korea's annual rainfall comes between June and September.

With the arrival of spring come swallows, migratory birds from the south, and the blossoming of forsythia, azalea, and cherry blossoms. The spring rains are crucial for preparing seedbeds for rice, sowing spring vegetables, and planting summer crops.

Autumn is a season of transition from the hot, humid summer weather to the cold, dry winter weather. During the autumn season, you can enjoy colorful autumn leaves everywhere in Korea, as seen in the picture below.

Figure 13.1: Autumn at 덕수궁 (Deoksu Palace) in Seoul, Korea.

Credit

Chapter 14. Making Plans for Vacation
크리스마스에 뭐 할 거예요?

Objectives

- You will be able to make plans for upcoming weekends/holidays/vacation.
- You will be able to exchange information with someone by asking and responding to questions about plans for next semester.
- You will be able to wish for a nice vacation/holiday.
- You will be able to describe your activities by using an appropriate tense according to the time frame of your activity.

Key Expressions and Structures

- V-(으)ㄹ 거예요: I will do V.
- [Time/day]에 뭐 할 거예요?: What are you going to do in/on/at [time/day]?
- 크리스마스/방학에 뭐 할 거예요?: What are you going to do on Christmas/vacation?
- [Day/time] 잘 보내세요!: Have a nice time during the [day/time]!
- 크리스마스/방학 잘 보내세요!: Merry Christmas! / Have a nice vacation!

Task: Make Plans for Christmas

Discuss your plans for winter break and what you are going to do for Christmas this year.

Practice Questions

1. 이번 겨울방학에 **뭐 할 거예요**?
2. 올해 크리스마스에 **뭐 할 거예요**?
3. 오늘 오후에 **뭐 할 거예요**?
4. **다음** 학기에 수업 몇 과목 **들을 거예요**?
5. **다음** 학기에 무슨 수업 **들을 거예요**?

Activity 1: 올해 크리스마스 계획을 세워 보세요.

What are you are going to do for Christmas this year? Do you have any plans for winter break?

Model Conversation

데이빗:	유진 씨, 겨울 방학에 집에 가세요?
김유진:	네, 기말 시험[22] 끝나고 집에 갈 거예요.
	데이빗 씨는 **겨울 방학에 뭐 할 거예요?**
데이빗:	네, 저도 집에 갈 거예요.
	가족들하고 크리스마스를 같이 보낼 거예요.
	유진 씨는 **크리스마스에 뭐 할 거예요?**
김유진:	저는 친구들하고 크리스마스 파티에 **갈 거예요**.
	보통 크리스마스에 고등학교 친구들을 만나요.
데이빗:	아, 그래요? 고등학교 친구들을 자주 만나요?
김유진:	아니요. 친구들이 많이 바빠요. 그래서 자주 못 만나요.
	이번 크리스마스에 파티도 하고 같이 영화도 **볼 거예요**.
데이빗:	그럼, **크리스마스 잘 보내세요!**
김유진:	네, 고마워요. 데이빗 씨도 **크리스마스 잘 보내세요!**

Your Own Conversation

A:	_____ 씨, 겨울 방학에 집에 가세요?
B:	네/아니요. _____.
	_____ 씨도 겨울 방학에 집에 가세요?
A:	네/아니요. 저도/는 _____.
	_____하고 크리스마스를 같이 보낼 거예요.
	(Who you are going to spend Christmas with?)
	_____ 씨는 크리스마스에 뭐 할 거예요?

---

[22] 기말 시험: final exam

B: _____

_____

(What you are going to do on Christmas.)

A: 아 그래요? _____

_____

(What you are going to do on Christmas.)

B: 그럼, _____!

(Have a Merry Christmas!)

A: _____씨도 _____!

(Have a Merry Christmas!)

Activity 2: 친구들의 다음 학기 계획에 대해서 인터뷰해 보세요.

Exchange information about your plans for next semester. Interview two classmates about how many/what kind of classes to take, where to live, with whom to live, if they will join a club, and so forth. Take notes of your interviews in the table and report it to the class.

Interview Questions

1. 다음 학기에 수업 몇 과목 들을 거예요?
2. 무슨 수업 들을 거예요? 다음 학기에도 한국어 수업 들을 거예요?
3. 다음 학기에 어디에서 살 거예요?
4. 다음 학기에 룸메이트하고 같이 살 거예요? 룸메이트는 누구예요?
5. 다음 학기에 동아리 활동 (club activity) 할 거예요?
6. 무슨 동아리 활동 할 거예요?

Interview Qs.	e.g. 에밀리	친구 1.	친구 2.
1.	4 과목		
2.	경제학, 생물학, 한국어 102 피아노		
3.	아파트		
4.	룸메이트: 제니, 생물학, 2 학년		
5. & 6.	댄싱 동호회		

Model Report

에밀리 씨는 다음 학기에 네 과목 들을 거예요. 경제학하고 생물학하고 한국어 수업을 들을 거예요. 이번 학기에는 기숙사에 살았어요. 그런데 다음 학기에는 룸메이트하고 아파트에서 살 거예요. 룸메이트는 제니예요. 제니는 생물학을 공부해요. 인디애나 대학교 2 학년이에요. 그리고 다음학기에 제니하고 같이 댄싱 동호회를 할 거예요. 제니도 저도 춤을 아주 좋아해요.

Your Report

_____

_____

_____

_____

_____

_____

Activity 3: 주말 저녁에 한 주에 일어났던 일들과 다음 주 계획을 일기에 써 보세요.

Suppose that it is a Sunday night, and you are writing a weekly diary. Write about what you did this weekend and your plans for next week. Be careful to use an appropriate tense, according to the time frame of your activity.

Model Writing

이번 주는 아주 바빴어요. 경제학 시험하고 한국어 시험이 있었어요. 그래서 매일 공부하러 도서관에 갔어요. 화요일에 경제학 시험을 보고 금요일에 한국어 시험을 봤어요. 경제학 시험이 아주 어려웠어요. 한국어 시험이 끝나고 반 친구들하고 한국 식당에 갔어요. 오래간만에 한국 음식을 먹었어요. 아주 맛있었어요.

다음 주에도 아마 바쁠 거예요. 한국어 말하기[23] 시험이 있어요. 그래서 연습하러 한국어 선생님 연구실에 갈 거예요. 주말에는 기숙사에서 할로윈 파티가 있어요. 이번 주

---

[23] 말하기: speaking

토요일이 10 월 31 일 할로윈 데이예요. 금요일에 룸메이트들하고 같이 파티 준비를 할 거예요.

Your Writing

_____

_____

_____

_____

_____

_____

_____

_____

토요일이 10 월 31 일 할로윈 데이예요. 금요일에 룸메이트들하고 같이 파티 준비를 할 거예요.

Cultural Awareness: Holidays in Korea 한국의 명절

There are two big holidays in Korea: one is 설날, New Year's Day, and the other is 추석, Harvest Festival. On 설날, New Year's Day, most Koreans celebrate a lunar new year. On 설날, people dress in 한복, Korean traditional clothes, and give a new year's bow 세배 to parents and grandparents, as shown in the picture below. When giving 세배, children say "새해 복 많이 받으세요!," which means "Get a lot of blessings on a new year!" After each bow, they receive money called 세뱃돈. A traditional dish for New Year's Day is 떡국, rice cake soup. You will get one year older only after you eat 떡국 on New Year's Day.

추석, Harvest Festival, is just like Thanksgiving Day in America. Many people go to their hometowns and visit with family. Around the time of 추석, all the highways and roads are packed with people driving to their hometowns. On 추석, people visit ancestors' graves to pay their respects and hold an ancestral rite called "차례." Special foods are prepared using newly harvested grains and produce, one of which is 송편, a kind of rice cake.

Figure 14.1: 세배 on New Year's Day.

Credit

- Fig. 14.1: Copyright © by Republic of Korea () at https://flic.kr/p/Dtktyb.

Appendix A

Chapter 2. Activity 2. Picture 1.

_____ 케빈 _____ 앨리사 _____ 리차드

_____ 스티븐 _____ 유진 _____ 수미

Chapter 2. Activity 2. Picture 2.

조나단 _____ 리나 _____ 마크 _____

앤 _____ 알렉스 _____ 캐서린 _____

Credits

- IMG 2.1a: Source: https://pixabay.com/en/books-library-education-literature-42701/.
- IMG 2.1b: Source: https://pixabay.com/en/umbrella-blue-rain-weather-158164/.
- IMG 2.1c: Source: https://pixabay.com/en/tumbler-milk-camping-1141198/.
- IMG 2.1d: Source: https://pixabay.com/en/headphones-auricle-transducer-375341/.
- IMG 2.1e: Source: https://pixabay.com/en/laptop-notebook-computer-black-158648/.
- IMG 2.1f: Source: https://pixabay.com/en/watch-wristwatch-wrist-watch-time-42803/.
- IMG 2.1g: Source: https://pixabay.com/en/purse-bag-strap-fashion-handbag-1051711/.
- IMG 2.1h: Source: https://pixabay.com/en/cap-baseball-hat-isolated-visor-304059/.
- IMG 2.1i: Source: https://pixabay.com/en/iphone-cellphone-smartphone-mobile-37856/.
- IMG 2.1j: Source: https://pixabay.com/en/dictionary-book-english-school-155951/.
- IMG 2.1k: Source: https://pixabay.com/en/data-transfer-connection-data-3199488/.
- IMG 2.1l: Source: https://pixabay.com/en/tablet-ipad-screen-internet-184888/.
- IMG 2.1a: Source: https://pixabay.com/en/books-library-education-literature-42701/.
- IMG 2.1b: Source: https://pixabay.com/en/umbrella-blue-rain-weather-158164/.
- IMG 2.1c: Source: https://pixabay.com/en/tumbler-milk-camping-1141198/.
- IMG 2.1d: Source: https://pixabay.com/en/headphones-auricle-transducer-375341/.
- IMG 2.1e: Source: https://pixabay.com/en/laptop-notebook-computer-black-158648/.
- IMG 2.1f: Source: https://pixabay.com/en/watch-wristwatch-wrist-watch-time-42803/.
- IMG 2.1g: Source: https://pixabay.com/en/purse-bag-strap-fashion-handbag-1051711/.
- IMG 2.1h: Source: https://pixabay.com/en/cap-baseball-hat-isolated-visor-304059/.
- IMG 2.1i: Source: https://pixabay.com/en/iphone-cellphone-smartphone-mobile-37856/.
- IMG 2.1j: Source: https://pixabay.com/en/dictionary-book-english-school-155951/.
- IMG 2.1k: Source: https://pixabay.com/en/data-transfer-connection-data-3199488/.
- IMG 2.1l: Source: https://pixabay.com/en/tablet-ipad-screen-internet-184888/.

Appendix B

Chapter 5. Activity 1. Picture 1.

제임스 _____ _____ 유진 _____ _____ 샘 _____

_____ 에릭 _____ 데이빗 _____

스캇 _____ 아담 _____ 미쉘 _____

Chapter 5. Activity 1. Picture 2.

_____ 에밀리 _____ 제니 _____

애니 _____ 레이첼 _____ 수지

_____ 마이클 _____ 크리스 _____

Credits

- IMG 5.1a: Source: https://pixabay.com/en/food-menu-glass-fruit-frisch-3324316/.
- IMG 5.1b: Source: https://pixabay.com/en/read-girl-reading-learn-child-3362482/.
- IMG 5.1c: Source: https://pixabay.com/en/cake-eat-food-sweet-eating-1746435/.
- IMG 5.1d: Copyright © by Elvert Barnes () at https://flic.kr/p/2nw2B.
- IMG 5.1e: Source: https://pixabay.com/en/children-tv-child-television-home-403582/.
- IMG 5.1f: Source: https://pixabay.com/en/child-children-happy-young-people-798740/.
- IMG 5.1g: Source: https://pixabay.com/en/blogging-blogger-office-business-336376/.
- IMG 5.1h: Source: https://pixabay.com/en/pizza-food-cheese-crust-pepperoni-2619491/.
- IMG 5.1i: Source: https://pixabay.com/en/sports-college-football-fans-990513/.
- IMG 5.1j: Source: https://pixabay.com/en/aroma-beverage-break-cafe-caffeine-3385067/.
- IMG 5.1k: Source: https://pixabay.com/en/homework-school-problem-number-2521144/
- IMG 5.1l: Source: https://pixabay.com/en/school-backpack-childhood-education-1634755/.
- IMG 5.1m: Source: https://pixabay.com/en/pokemon-pokemongo-friends-school-1548194/.
- IMG 5.1n: Source: https://pixabay.com/en/university-lecture-campus-education-105709/.
- IMG 5.1o: Source: https://pixabay.com/en/white-sheet-bed-room-people-girl-2565766/.
- IMG 5.1a: Source: https://pixabay.com/en/food-menu-glass-fruit-frisch-3324316/.
- IMG 5.1b: Source: https://pixabay.com/en/read-girl-reading-learn-child-3362482/.
- IMG 5.1c: Source: https://pixabay.com/en/cake-eat-food-sweet-eating-1746435/.
- IMG 5.1d: Copyright © by Elvert Barnes () at https://flic.kr/p/2nw2B.
- IMG 5.1e: Source: https://pixabay.com/en/children-tv-child-television-home-403582/.
- IMG 5.1f: Source: https://pixabay.com/en/child-children-happy-young-people-798740/.
- IMG 5.1g: Source: https://pixabay.com/en/blogging-blogger-office-business-336376/.
- IMG 5.1h: Source: https://pixabay.com/en/pizza-food-cheese-crust-pepperoni-2619491/.
- IMG 5.1i: Source: https://pixabay.com/en/sports-college-football-fans-990513/.
- IMG 5.1j: Source: https://pixabay.com/en/aroma-beverage-break-cafe-caffeine-3385067/.
- IMG 5.1k: Source: https://pixabay.com/en/homework-school-problem-number-2521144/.
- IMG 5.1l: Source: https://pixabay.com/en/school-backpack-childhood-education-1634755/.
- IMG 5.1m: Source: https://pixabay.com/en/pokemon-pokemongo-friends-school-1548194/.
- IMG 5.1n: Source: https://pixabay.com/en/university-lecture-campus-education-105709/.
- IMG 5.1o: Source: https://pixabay.com/en/white-sheet-bed-room-people-girl-2565766/.

CPSIA information can be obtained
at www.ICGtesting.com
Printed in the USA
LVHW020454060822
725256LV00004B/20